MODERN COMBAT AIRCRAFT

MODERN COMBAT AIRCRAFT

Bill Gunston

TREASURE PRESS

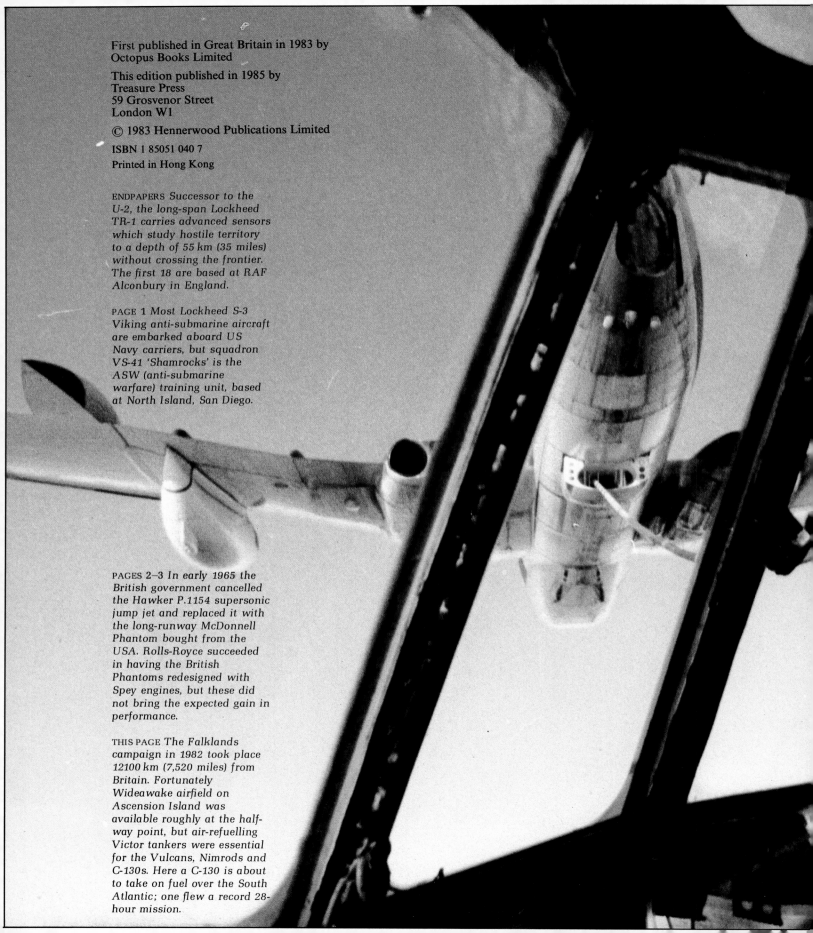

First published in Great Britain in 1983 by
Octopus Books Limited

This edition published in 1985 by
Treasure Press
59 Grosvenor Street
London W1

ISBN 1 85051 040 7

Printed in Hong Kong

ENDPAPERS *Successor to the
U-2, the long-span Lockheed
TR-1 carries advanced sensors
which study hostile territory
to a depth of 55 km (35 miles)
without crossing the frontier.
The first 18 are based at RAF
Alconbury in England.*

PAGE 1 *Most Lockheed S-3
Viking anti-submarine aircraft
are embarked aboard US
Navy carriers, but squadron
VS-41 'Shamrocks' is the
ASW (anti-submarine
warfare) training unit, based
at North Island, San Diego.*

PAGES 2–3 *In early 1965 the
British government cancelled
the Hawker P.1154 supersonic
jump jet and replaced it with
the long-runway McDonnell
Phantom bought from the
USA. Rolls-Royce succeeded
in having the British
Phantoms redesigned with
Spey engines, but these did
not bring the expected gain in
performance.*

THIS PAGE *The Falklands
campaign in 1982 took place
12100 km (7,520 miles) from
Britain. Fortunately
Wideawake airfield on
Ascension Island was
available roughly at the half-
way point, but air-refuelling
Victor tankers were essential
for the Vulcans, Nimrods and
C-130s. Here a C-130 is about
to take on fuel over the South
Atlantic; one flew a record 28-
hour mission.*

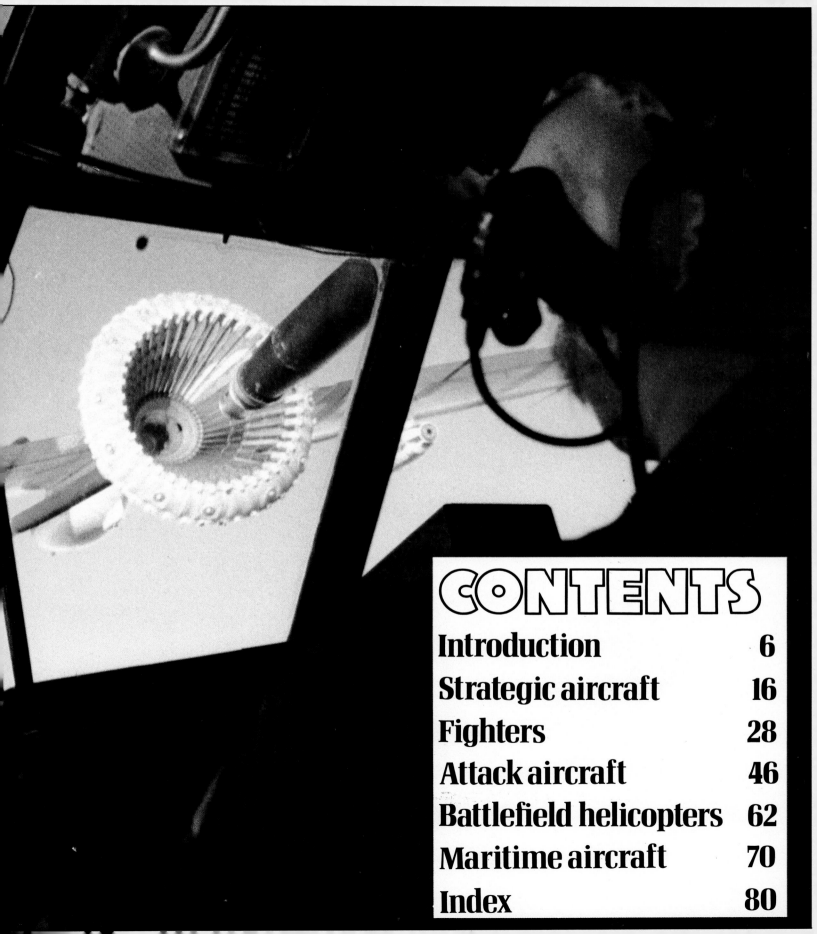

CONTENTS

INTRODUCTION

PRECEDING PAGES *The de Havilland Aircraft company created the 'wooden wonder' Mosquito in the teeth of official opposition, flying the prototype in November 1940. It proved to be faster than any RAF fighter, and 40 versions were built for almost every military purpose. These B.IV Srs 2 bombers were pictured with 139 Sqn, the second to receive Mosquitoes, in 1942. The squadron's first combat mission was a lunch-time raid on the Philips factory at Eindhoven in the Netherlands on 20 November 1942.*

At the start of World War 1, in August 1914, the aeroplane was only just beginning to develop into a practical vehicle. Previously it had been a very hit-and-miss affair, and at least half the early would-be aviators failed to get off the ground. Once in the air, early aeroplanes were extremely unreliable, and their performance was so low that even a slight headwind was serious. On the ground their frailty was ill-suited to the rough environment of a military campaign. Not least, there was no organized method of teaching people how to fly, and for most of the war the casualty rate among pupil pilots was appalling.

By 1918 aeroplanes were still dangerous to their crews as well as to their enemies, but progress had been remarkable. In just over four years of war the speed of aircraft had doubled, from 100 km/h (62 mph) to 200 km/h (124 mph). Engine reliability had improved greatly, although by modern standards it was still poor. Whereas in 1914 the general official view was that there was no role for the aeroplane in warfare, except conceivably to carry a reconnaissance observer, when peace returned thousands of aircraft had been built for air combat, bombing, torpedo dropping, submarine hunting, correcting the fire of friendly artillery, destroying airships, co-operating with surface fleets and many other roles, including the protective escort of other aircraft. Night flying had become routine, although high winds and heavy rain or snow could keep aircraft on the ground — where not infrequently they were blown upside-down in gales and severely damaged.

In the ten years after World War 1 aircraft increased in weight, engine power and reliability, but basically the changes were minimal. The standard fighter armament remained two machine guns, synchronized with the rotation of the engine so that the bullets could not shoot off the blades of the propeller. Bombers continued

RIGHT *The famed British Sopwith Camel shot down about 3,000 enemy machines, far more than any other aircraft of World War 1.*

to fly at a mere 200 km/h (124 mph), and aim externally hung bombs by a somewhat crude geometrical sight which a skilled handyman could have made at home. Although an international race for the Schneider Trophy, held every two years, resulted in seaplanes capable of flying at more than 700 km/h (435 mph), the seaplanes actually used by air forces could not manage more than 200 km/h. Even the fastest landplane fighters could only reach less than 300 km/h (186 mph) as late as the early 1930s.

Then engineers in Germany and the USA introduced all-metal stressed-skin construction, in which a thin skin of aluminium was used instead of wood or fabric. This skin was strong enough to bear a large part of the structural loads, so it was possible to make wings thinner, change from biplanes to monoplanes and do away with bracing struts and thus reduce drag (wind resistance). Drag was further reduced by enclosing engines in carefully designed cowlings which gave the whole aircraft a more streamlined shape without causing the engine to overheat. The invention of slats – long curved

strips which at low speeds could be extended a few inches from the leading edge of the wing – enabled aircraft to fly safely with much smaller wings, or alternatively to fly at much slower speeds and get in and out of small fields even when heavily loaded. Not all aircraft used slats, but another invention, the flap, had by World War 2 in September 1939 become almost universal. Usually much larger than slats, flaps are auxiliary surfaces hinged down or extended from the underside of the wing near the trailing edge. When partly extended they increase the lift, and so enable the aircraft to fly slower without dropping out of the sky. When fully down they greatly increase drag. Thus flaps might be put part-way down for take-off and fully down for landing.

Other inventions (which dated from before 1921 but only became common after the mid-1930s) were the variable-pitch propeller and retractable landing gear. The former enabled the angular setting of the propeller blades to be adjusted to a fine pitch for take-off, when a high engine speed (for maximum power) had to be

ABOVE *This modern aircraft is an exact replica of an Albatros D.Va, one of the best German fighters of the 1917–18 period. Almost all German aircraft were powered by water-cooled engines with one row of six cylinders, in this case giving about 185 hp.*

ABOVE *Two of the most famous Allied fighters of 1944 flying together almost 40 years later. Adrian Swire's beautifully restored Spitfire IX in the background is often seen at air shows. Nearer the camera is a P-51D Mustang, designed five years after the Spitfire and able to fly twice as far and at higher speed on an identical Rolls-Royce Merlin engine!*

reconciled with low airspeed, and then pivot the blades to a coarse pitch for high-speed flight, when despite high airspeed the engine could run quite slowly for best fuel consumption. The retractable landing gear offered a significant reduction in drag, which increased the effective range of bomber and reconnaissance aircraft and improved the combat performance of fighters.

Perhaps surprisingly, many pilots did not like the new breed of all-metal monoplanes, with their enclosed cockpits and many new devices. They felt the traditional fabric-covered biplane would be less prone to go wrong, easier to fly, offer much better pilot view in all directions and be more agile in combat; and it was certainly better suited to the small grass airfields. But nothing could stand in the way of the much greater speed, range, firepower, bombload and fighting ability of the strong yet much more streamlined monoplanes. Despite their great

cost they were the aircraft that fought World War 2, and all over the world good new airfields with 2000m (2,200-yard) paved runways were built to enable this airpower to be provided.

World War 2 (1939–45) saw aircraft used in much greater numbers than at any time before or since. A very small proportion, such as the Fairey Swordfish of Britain's Fleet Air Arm, were of the old fabric-covered biplane type. On the Russian front a 1927 trainer, the Po-2, was used as a front-line combat machine with guns and light bombs, although it could not reach much beyond 100 km/h (62 mph) when laden. The Luftwaffe which opposed it scoured the training schools for similar early biplane trainers such as the Fw 44, He 72 and Go 145; all of these were used in hundreds for front-line combat. These were chosen because of the demand for extreme simplicity and reliability in the most harsh conditions, and the ability to carry military loads safely from small aircraft

smaller engines and came off second-best. The Americans perfected turbochargers, devices driven by the hot exhaust gas from the engine to pump in extra fresh air and thus increase power at great heights. These were used in fighters like the P-38 Lightning and P-47 Thunderbolt, and also in such famous heavy bombers as the B-17 Flying Fortress and B-24 Liberator.

By 1944 a much more advanced US heavy bomber, the B-29 Superfortress, was in service in the Far East. It had two turbos on each of its four giant 2,200 hp engines, and was as fast as many fighters at high altitudes 10 km (33,000 ft) from the ground. Here the air is very thin, and as well as having oxygen the B-29 crew was enclosed in sealed pressure cabins which were pumped up with fresh air to keep the interior more like that at sea level. The B-29 also had five power-driven turrets armed with heavy machine guns and cannon, aimed by gunners elsewhere in the aircraft linked to the turrets by complex remote-control systems. The B-29 showed that military aircraft were going to become even more complicated and expensive, but for speed, height and above all range (distance flown) with a heavy bombload, the B-29 was in a class by itself.

It was the B-29 that dropped atomic bombs on Japan in August 1945 to bring the war to an end. The development of such nuclear weapons changed warfare dramatically. Suddenly a single bomber could destroy a city, a task previously needing hundreds, and this greatly complicated the job of defending radars and fighters. Another problem was jet propulsion, which reached the RAF and Luftwaffe in the summer of 1944. Although it resulted in faster fighters it also increased the speed of bombers by an even greater amount. In fact when in 1951 the RAF introduced the twin-jet Canberra it had a bomber, able to drop atom bombs, which could fly faster and higher, and even turn better, than any of its fighters!

Yet jet propulsion was not the answer to everything. When the Korean War broke out in 1950 the main need was for aircraft to fly attack missions against powerful invading armies. The jet fighters, such as the F-80 Shooting Star, F-84 Thunderjet and the US Navy/Marines F9F Panther and F2H Banshee, could all reach nearly 1000 km/h (620 mph) but they carried very few bombs or rockets, needed long smoothly paved runways and could not fly longer than about an hour and a half. The carrier-based A-1 Skyraider, with a B-29 type piston engine, was much slower but it could use rough airstrips, carry several tonnes of bombs and fly as long as nine hours non-stop at low level. It was realized that someone had to build a versatile attack aircraft able to fly Skyraider missions but at jet speed. It was also appreciated that it should be fitted with advanced electronic devices to enable it to navigate by night or in very bad weather and then quickly find difficult targets – such as a bridge, enemy encampment or large group of trucks hidden in a forest – and deliver weapons accurately against them.

carriers or restricted front-line bases and get to close grips with the enemy. Not unnaturally, these very slow aircraft were shot down in droves, but they represented a recognition of the often-forgotten fact that for many missions high speed is almost a handicap. Today quite slow aircraft are being made for attacking enemy troops and tanks engaged in land battles, while others are built for missions over the ocean, as described later.

For air combat, however, the highest possible performance was essential. High engine power was needed mainly for superiority in rate of climb and better manoeuvrability, although sheer speed was useful in catching an enemy or escaping from an engagement if necessary (when out of ammunition, for example). In 1940 the British Hurricane and Spitfire, with engines of over 1,000 horsepower (hp), defeated the German fighters, while those of France, Italy and other European nations struggled with

ABOVE *The Hawker Hurricane was by far the most important British fighter in the first two years of World War 2, which included the Battle of Britain. This example is still flying, but unfortunately has incorrect Spitfire-type exhaust stubs, six on each side, instead of three larger ones.*

Even today this attack or interdiction mission is very difficult to accomplish. As late as the Vietnam war, which reached its tragic peak in 1965–73, most Allied aircraft were unsuited to the job. The fighters were designed to fly at Mach 2 (twice the speed of sound) at heights of more than 10 km (33,000 ft), and armed with large radar-guided missiles to enable them to shoot down enemy aircraft at a range of about 30 km (19 miles). (Mach number is the scale used for the speed of fast aircraft relative to the speed of sound.) But the US government told fighter pilots to make positive identification of every aircraft before opening fire, and this involved closing to only a few hundred metres, at which the Communist MiGs with their greater agility

and close-range missiles and cannon were at a great advantage. Many US fighters could not meet the need, and even the best type, the big F-4 Phantom, had to be modified hurriedly with a slat (an automatically opened curved strip along the front of the wing) to improve its manoeuvrability and a cannon to help it kill at close range.

As for the attack mission, the best aircraft were at first built for the US Navy. The small and agile A-4 Skyhawk, the big A-6 Intruder and versatile A-7 Corsair II were given all the systems and devices needed to fly from carrier decks or small airfields while carrying bombloads up to 6800 kg (15,000 lb), and to navigate in all conditions and drop bombs on very difficult targets with great accuracy. The USAF wanted a new fighter in 1960 and bought the F-111, a monster aircraft with such new devices as afterburning turbofan engines (giving huge power with good fuel economy) and pivoted swing-wings (so that the wings could be spread out for take-off, slow flying and landing, and folded back like an arrow for supersonic flight). However, the F-111 was not very successful as a fighter because it was so big and heavy, but it proved to be a superb long-range attack aircraft with the vital ability to fly straight to a small ground target and drop a bomb accurately on it at jet speed.

The F-111 also introduced another new device, the TFR (terrain-following radar). The development of radar gave defenders the ability to 'see' enemy aircraft at great distances, even at night or in bad weather, and to guide fighters or other defences (such as guns or missiles) to shoot them down. Until about 1950 it was usually thought that future bomber or attack aircraft should be made as fast and high-flying as possible; thus, it was thought, they would be more difficult to shoot down. But the development of improved radars and deadly SAMs (surface-to-air missiles) soon showed that any high-flying aircraft could be blown out of the sky with 100 per cent certainty. The only other alternative was to fly as low as possible, even though this meant flying rather slower, and also reduced range by greatly increasing the fuel consumption. Thus, with the help of modern electronic devices and decoys, and a fair amount of luck, attack aircraft can even now penetrate defended airspace and prove very hard to shoot

down. Even with radars on towers and hilltops the problem of detecting and accurately firing on a fast jet at treetop height is still not completely overcome (if it were, most air force squadrons might as well be disbanded!).

The F-111 was the first of the new breed of attack aircraft with terrain-following radar in which the ability to hug the ground is their main key to survival. One has only to fly in the side-by-side cockpit of an F-111 to realize it is at once the most thrilling and terrifying ride imaginable. Even on a fine day roaring at full throttle across flat farmland is exciting, with the aircraft constantly weaving up, down, left and right to avoid rising ground, cottages, trees and such obstructions as radio masts and electricity cables. Flying a mission in mountains shrouded in cloud is absolutely terrifying to the inexperienced passenger. The aircraft pulls violently up the face of an invisible mountain, breasts the ridge at the top and plunges violently down towards what seems to be the centre of the Earth. It takes strong nerves not to take over the controls and pull up to heights far removed from the jagged rocks! This terrain-following mode is adopted by all advanced modern attack aircraft fitted with TFR, while the simpler machines have to fly as low as possible manually (under direct pilot control).

At Suez in November 1956 British and French jets combined with the new air force of Israel in ground attack missions which, in the main, were no different from those of World War 2. But large jet bombers, such as the Vickers Valiant and the Canberra, were used for the first time,

BELOW *Although the 12,731 built was far surpassed by the amazing production of 19,203 B-24 Liberators (including equivalent spares) the Boeing B-17 Fortress was much more famous as the chief US bomber of World War 2. This B-17E of early 1942 was one of the first built of a redesigned version with greatly enhanced defensive firepower which was to be tested to the limit in the skies over Germany.*

demonstrating great accuracy in high-level bombing under radar guidance, the radar in the aircraft taking the place of the optical bomb-sight. In the later Arab/Israeli wars of 1967 and 1973 the guided AAM (air-to-air missile) became the dominant fighter weapon, with the ability to kill with almost total efficiency from considerable distances. On the other hand, these conflicts in the blue sunlit skies of the Middle East did little to provide NATO with the experience and mentality needed for modern warfare in really bad weather.

Both the Korean (1950–53) and Vietnam wars (1962–73) did involve prolonged operations in bad weather, and both emphasized repeatedly the vital need for attack aircraft able to place ordnance accurately on ground targets under the most adverse conditions. But for most of the time these wars were waged by aircraft totally unsuited to the task in hand. As in Korea the choice in Vietnam often seemed to be fast jets with little bombload, range or endurance, but good ability to evade defences, and propeller-driven aircraft with excellent bombload, range and endurance but highly vulnerable to ground fire. The USAF spent enormous sums building up giant airbases on the island of Guam and in Thailand for use by the colossal B-52 eight-jet strategic bomber. This had been designed to

drop nuclear bombs on major targets such as cities, and had only a limited conventional bombload. Large numbers were completely re-built to carry enormous loads of ordinary bombs (up to about 38 tonnes) which were then rained down on areas of forest where enemy troops were thought to be hiding. Any less economic way of waging war would be hard to imagine. Even if every mission had found Viet Cong soldiers, with rifles and bicycles, actually present in the attacked area (which they mostly were not), a profit/loss account of the operation would have looked ludicrous. Later the B-52s were used to bomb more genuine targets, such as factories and airfields, but by the 1970s the Viet Cong defences had become the strongest in the world, and numerous B-52s were shot down by SAMs, even though the missiles used were of a very old and primitive type.

What Vietnam did do was to spur the development of a new breed of close-support aircraft designed to be based among forward troops and fly missions on the direct orders of those troops, knocking out enemy armour, fortifications and other tough centres of resistance which friendly troops were finding hard to overcome. In Algeria, in the long and bitter war that gave that country independence, the French had pioneered the use of relatively low-powered

BELOW *The Avro Lancaster came about by chance: the original twin-engined Manchester was a failure and Avro turned it into the Lancaster by fitting four of the reliable Merlin engines. It was by far the most important RAF heavy bomber of World War 2.*

(mostly propeller-driven) aeroplanes and helicopters as close-support aircraft armed with bombs, rockets, wire-guided missiles, cannon and machine guns. In Vietnam the use of close-support aircraft was taken further, with helicopters used as 'air cavalry' on reconnaissance and troop-carrying missions, and with heavily armed helicopters used as escorts and in the anti-tank role. More than in any other war, FACs (forward air controllers) were used in various types of piston or jet aircraft orbiting a ground target and by voice radio giving attacking aircraft exact instructions on how best to make an accurate attack. Many previously unknown species of combat aircraft were used, including air-refuelling tankers, airborne command posts, large long-endurance electronic-warfare aircraft (of many sub-types, used for such tasks as monitoring enemy radio and radar signals, or picking up and analysing signals from sensitive vibration sensors dropped to detect the passage of hostile trucks), and even large cargo transports bristling with electronic sensors and guns of various calibres and used to blast hidden ground targets by night.

Today several of these classes have ceased to exist. In the following pages all the most important modern combat aircraft are discussed and their performance assessed.

ABOVE *The Boeing B-52 eight-jet heavy bomber was designed to drop single nuclear weapons on distant cities from high in the stratosphere. In Vietnam it became a 'trucking system' for delivering up to 40 tonnes of high explosive to random areas of forest!*

LEFT *Another type put to uses totally unlike those its designers had in mind is the McDonnell F-4 Phantom II. It was created as a carrier-based fighter for the US Navy, but this F-4E of the US Air Force is showering bombs over Vietnam.*

STRATEGIC AIRCRAFT

Until World War 2 the basic limitations of aircraft performance made it impossible for bombers, or even reconnaïssance aircraft carrying no load but a few cameras, to fly missions longer than such trips as Britain to Berlin and back, or Britain to North Africa. Even these were regarded as a stern test of man and machine, and airpower had to be confined to a single area of operations. To get aircraft to a different part of the world, such as from an American factory to West Africa or from Britain to India, invariably meant shipment by sea.

Gradual development of aircraft with much greater range came in parallel with jet propulsion, but the higher fuel consumption of the new jets made long-range performance more difficult. Thus when the USAF formed Strategic Air Command in March 1946 all its early equipment was piston-engined. The mighty B-36, in some ways the biggest combat aircraft of all time, was

ABOVE *The Soviet Union has a great tradition of very large aircraft, but it was still a major engineering achievement when the Tupolev team created the Tu-95 (which NATO calls the 'Bear'). Although powered by enormous turboprops, for good fuel economy over global distances, it has swept wings and tail, and can fly at jet speeds. Many are over 25 years old.*

RIGHT *Smaller than the Tu-95, and powered by two very large turbojets at the roots of the wing, the Tu-88 is known to NATO as 'Badger'. This example is serving with Egypt, and carries two 'Kelt' anti-ship missiles.*

PRECEDING PAGES *Some of the most striking aircraft photographs of recent years have been taken by boom operators of USAF tanker aircraft. Here fuel is about to be supplied to a Boeing B-52D, the type which bore the brunt of the long conventional warfare missions in Vietnam.*

designed to bomb Germany from the USA and return, and thus it had for the first time what could be called 'global' striking power. With it came nuclear weapons, and a new concept was born: deterrence. Whereas previous bombers had been built to fight wars, SAC bombers were intended mainly to prevent a war from ever starting.

By 1965 the deterrent task was fast being assigned to two new weapons, the land-based ICBM (intercontinental ballistic missile) and the SLBM (submarine-launched ballistic missile). In both these new categories initial US dominance was quickly overtaken by the Soviet Union, and renewal of US deterrent forces has been overdue for many years. It seems beyond belief that the newest SAC strategic bomber is the B-52, which flew in 1952, and the newest ICBM the Minuteman, which was launched in 1961. However, orders have now been placed for the new B1-B

bomber (see page 26), and the controversial Peacekeeper (MX) missile is under review.

In the late 1950s there was general belief, which even extended to a few experts, that bombers as a class were obsolete. ICBMs and SLBMs were thought to be so much harder to stop that many people overlooked their several shortcomings. One is that a missile is efficient as a delivery system only for a nuclear warhead against a fixed target such as a city or airfield. It is very poor at carrying heavy loads of conventional high explosive, or in attacking moving targets such as ships or armies. Even more crucial is the fact that a missile cannot be recalled. The first indication of full-scale aggression by a major power would be the appearance of numerous objects on defending radar screens with the characteristics of ICBM or SLBM warheads. No government in the West would dare order a retaliatory missile strike at this stage; but to wait for the incoming warheads to hit would be to risk losing one's own missile force. Bombers, on the other hand, could be launched as soon as the warning was given of what looked on radar like an enemy attack. If there was any mistake, they could safely be recalled.

The only strategic nuclear powers having this choice are the Soviet Union, USA, France and probably China. In addition, Britain has four nuclear ballistic-missile submarines, at least one of which is always at sea, but this alone is hardly a viable deterrent. The Royal Navy would prefer five of these submarines, so that two could always be kept at sea. A deterrent force which appears to be ineffectual, or backed by a government that in a crisis might back down, is no longer a deterrent and might as well not exist.

Nobody has ever doubted the political will of the Kremlin, so the gigantic strategic forces of the Soviet Union are taken very seriously indeed. Their thousands of long-range missiles, both land- and sea-based, are outside the scope of this book. The Soviet bombers are divided roughly evenly between the DA (long-range aviation of the air force) and the AVMF (naval air force). Both have large nuclear capability, but the Russian AVMF long-range aircraft are assigned more varied missions including co-operation with surface fleets, electronic warfare and reconnaissance, and ASW (anti-submarine warfare).

Although an old design the Tu-95 or Tu-142, called 'Bear' by NATO, remains an important aircraft in both the DA and AVMF. It is a unique example of a swept-wing turboprop, with speed similar to that of most long-range jets. Thanks to the use of four monster engines, each of over 11 MW (15,000 hp), driving eight-blade contra-rotating propellers, these extremely large and impressive machines can carry 73000 litres (16,000 gallons) of kerosene fuel, which – thanks to the economy of turboprop propulsion – gives a range of some 13000 km (8,000 miles) and an endurance of 25 hours. These classic aircraft were still being built in small numbers in the early 1980s, and many of the earlier machines have been in service 25 years and flown many thousands of hours. One of the older versions, called 'Bear-B', was equipped to launch an extremely large cruise missile which NATO staffs believe is an anti-ship weapon. Most aircraft of this family are used today for various forms of maritime reconnaissance and ASW, ranging right across the globe from Soviet bases and often operating from such countries as Cuba and Somalia.

The rival to the Tu-95 in the early 1950s was the M-4, from the Myasishchyev design bureau, a broadly similar aircraft but powered by four large turbojets at the roots of the wing. When the M-4 was designed it was almost impossible to make jet aircraft fly the long ranges demanded. and the M-4 has never had quite the same range as the 'Bear' family, and its endurance is limited to about 15 hours (still no mean

figure for a jet designed 30 years ago). Like the rival Tupolev machines the M-4 has most of its crew housed in a pressurized compartment in the nose, with a gunner in the tail who, with other crew members, directs the fire of powerful remotely sighted gun turrets. Those in the most common M-4 version, called 'Bison-A' by NATO, mount a total of ten 23 mm cannon, the heaviest defensive armament of any regular combat aircraft. An estimated 43 M-4s were in use in 1983 as bombers, and about another 30 were employed as air-refuelling tankers.

Most numerous of all Soviet strategic aircraft were the Tu-16 family, known to NATO as 'Badger', of which some 2,000 were made. At the same time a similar number was built of the USAF B-47 Stratojet, with roughly comparable capability, but the last B-47 was withdrawn in 1967. In contrast at least 1,000 Badgers remain in active service, and they have been built or modified in at least 11 major versions for bombing, several forms of reconnaissance, tanking, electronic warfare and as a carrier of large cruise missiles. The basic Tu-16 is smaller than the 'Bear' and 'Bison', and powered by two large

---

Tupolev 'Backfire-B' (Tu-22M ?)
Country of origin: Soviet Union.
Dimensions and weights: Wingspan, 20°: 34·45 m (113 ft 0 in), 65°: 26·21 m (86 ft 0 in); length 40·23 m (132 ft 0 in); maximum loaded weight 122500 kg (270,000 lb).
Engines: Four Kuznetsov NK-144 augmented turbofans—believed to be 20000 kg (44,090 lb).
Maximum speed: 2124 km/h (1,320 mph).
Range: At high altitude 11000 km (6,835 miles).
Military load: Up to 3 AS-4 'Kitchen' or AS-6 'Kingfish' missiles, or up to 12000 kg (26,455 lb) of bombs; unknown external load.

turbojets at the wing-roots (the same basic type of engines as used in the M-4) can fly about 5000 km (3,100 miles), or for a maximum of about 8 hours. Recent versions have been seen carrying long-range supersonic missiles, of types known to NATO as AS-4 'Kitchen' and AS-6 'Kingfish', carried either on wing pylons or under the fuselage.

All these quite old Soviet aircraft represented great technical achievements when they were designed more than 30 years ago. At that time many comparable Western aircraft were being produced which, for reasons of engine life, structural fatigue or other deficiences, have not flown operationally for many years. Of course, we in the West do not know what effort and cost may have been needed to keep these tired old airframes combat-ready; all indications are that they have borne the strain remarkably well.

The giant Soviet M-50 supersonic bomber of 1959 never entered service, mainly because — like most early supersonic aircraft — it was deficient in range. By the 1960s, however, useful strategic missions could be flown by supersonic aircraft, and the Tupolev bureau took on the challenge. In the late 1950s its designers created the Tu-22 'Blinder', first seen at an airshow in 1961. Like many Tupolev machines its four-wheel main landing gears fold backwards into large streamlined boxes projecting behind the wing, and another distinctive feature is the placing of the two very large afterburning turbojets above the rear fuselage, where they merge into each side of the fin. (Afterburning is a

BELOW The predecessor of 'Backfire' was the Tu-22 'Blinder', a massive supersonic bomber that first flew before 1961. Here ground crew pose beside one of the enormous afterburning turbojet engines which can propel the 84-tonne machine at 1480 km/h (920 mph).

ABOVE *Since December 1982 B-52G heavy bombers of the USAF Strategic Air Command have been converted to carry cruise missiles (of a different type from the controversial land-based cruise missile). Here the 12 missiles can be seen hung on external racks. Later in the 1980s the aircraft will be modified to carry a further 8 missiles internally.*

method of boosting engine thrust by burning extra fuel in the jetpipe downstream of the rest of the engine.) It gives greatly enhanced thrust for take-off or supersonic flight, but at the expense of severely increased fuel consumption. Thus, it is avoided during a mission if possible, unless range is no problem and there will be plenty of spare fuel.

Like the other Soviet strategic machines the Tu-22 exists in several versions, but all have a crew of three in the nose and a remotely directed 23 mm cannon in the tail, just beneath the engine nozzles. Some versions are bombers, some missile carriers and one is a versatile reconnaissance type packed with electronics and cameras and used mainly on maritime missions. Initial Western estimates of the Tu-22's performance were ridiculously wide of the mark (it is common Western practice to under-value Soviet aircraft until the true figures emerge). Range was generally estimated as 2250 km (1,400 miles), but the correct figure is about 6500 km (4,000 miles), and even with a 400 km (250-mile) supersonic dash the Tu-22 can

fly to a target 2800 km (1,750 miles) distant and return. Nevertheless, even 6500 km is marginal for most Soviet strategic purposes and only about 250 of these otherwise fine aircraft were built. They are used by both the DA and AVMF, and a few are in service in Iraq and Libya; aircraft of the latter country are the only strategic supersonic bombers to see action (over Tanzania and Chad).

In the 1960s the Tupolev designers developed a swing-wing version of 'Blinder' designated Tu-22M (M probably meaning 'modified'), with greater fuel capacity and more powerful engines. NATO called the new bomber 'Backfire', but only a limited number entered service before production changed to a further developed version known in the West as 'Backfire-B'. This has no projecting fairings behind the wings; instead the new multi-wheel main landing gears retract inwards. Thanks to the pivoted outer wings the maximum weight at take-off has been considerably increased, from about 84 tonnes to some 123 tonnes, and as most of the increase is fuel the maximum range has gone up to well over 8000 km (5,000 miles). Like all other Soviet strategic aircraft, Backfire-B has an inflight-refuelling probe with which endurance can be extended to the limit the crew can stand. Already these extremely useful supersonic machines range widely over the Atlantic and Pacific, Indian Ocean and other sea areas, although by late 1982 none had been spotted operating from a foreign base and certainly none had then been exported.

The Soviet government stated in the SALT 2 (Strategic Arms Limitation Talks) treaty negotiations in 1979 that Backfires were tactical rather than strategic aircraft, lacking the capability to make an unrefuelled bombing mission to most of the USA from Soviet territory and return. The refuelling probes were removed from aircraft in service at this time, but of course they could be replaced in minutes and indeed soon reappeared after the negotiations were abandoned. Most of these aircraft are equipped to carry 'Kitchen' or 'Kingfish' missiles, as well as heavy loads of bombs and other stores in an internal bay and on external racks under the large engine inlet ducts. At high altitude Backfire-B is estimated to be able to fly at Mach 2, although in actual warfare it would be unlikely to fly higher than 100 m (325 ft), at which the speed has to be subsonic. Tail guns are fitted, as in Tu-22, but the most important defences for aircraft in this class are electronic. Numerous installations are pro-

vided for detecting hostile radars and other emissions, warning the crew of any which are dangerous (especially those associated with SAM guidance), transmitting jamming or specially composed radio emissions to cause the enemy defenders the maximum confusion, and also for ejecting packaged payloads such as chaff, flares or small radio jammers let down very slowly by parachute in the wake of the speeding bomber. Not the least important feature of Backfire-B is that it has been in production since about 1974 and the number in service by early 1983 was estimated at 300.

In the late 1970s satellite photographs taken by the USA began to show a prototype of a much larger and more powerful Tupolev swing-wing bomber which eventually, in 1982, was given the name 'Blackjack'. Its true designation is not yet known, but it looks extremely similar to the American B-1 (see page 26), but is rather larger and more powerful. It is probably powered by the same engines as used in the Tu-144 or -144D SST (supersonic transports), either the 20-tonne thrust NK-144 afterburning turbofan or the even more advanced Koliesov variable-bypass engine used in the -144D. Maximum weight of the new Soviet bomber is probably about 220 tonnes, roughly the same as the B-1, so with larger wings and more powerful engines it should be able to use shorter runways. This is an important consideration in the design of strategic

BELOW *The only USAF bombers less than 20 years old are the small force of FB-111s, a version of a tactical attack aircraft lacking the range for strategic missions. Capable of carrying four small SRAM (short-range attack missiles) under the wings, they can fly about 2900 km (1,800 miles) to a target and return. This FB from the 509th Bomb Wing was photographed when it wore the winged-2 badge of the 2nd Air Force, which was later disbanded.*

BELOW *In the late 1940s Britain planned three kinds of long-range jet bomber, the Valiant, Victor and Vulcan. The Valiant saw action at Suez in 1956 but none of the others went to war until, within a few weeks of their final retirement in April 1982, the Vulcans were suddenly called upon to bomb the airfield at Port Stanley in the Falklands. Vulcans similar to this one flew tough 16-hour missions on 12800 km (8,000-mile) round trips from the airbase on Ascension Island, the longest in the history of warfare.*

bombers, because unless they can spend their active lives dispersed among hundreds of minor airfields they run the grave risk of being destroyed by a nuclear missile on their own base. The only alternative is to keep a crew on board each aircraft with the bomber 'cocked' (ready for instant engine start), so that it can get away from the neighbourhood of the base and out to a safe distance in the two or three minutes that might be given before an enemy missile attack.

In 1983 few details of 'Blackjack' were known in the West, although a hazy and distorted electronically transmitted picture of it (taken by satellite) had been published showing a prototype parked near to Tu-144 SSTs. Unlike the Western democracies the Soviet regime is not prone to any change of government, and long-range bomber prototypes are not built and then cancelled because of a change of policy. Obviously there may be problems in developing this impressive new bomber, but the West would be foolish to count on it.

The trouble with major weapon systems in a democracy is that they take far longer to develop than the life of any elected government. Thus, while they are still years from service, a fresh administration may arrive determined to transfer funds to something else and the weapon programme is cancelled (as happened to more than 70 per cent of major British weapon programmes in 1950–65). This not only wastes money but disperses design teams, shatters morale and degrades the nation's ability either to defend itself or make its own weapons. Even the wealthy USA has not been immune to these problems, and the sheer cost of building a new strategic aircraft made this one of the first and biggest casualties. Trying to build a successor to the B-52 has proved one of the most difficult projects the USA has ever attempted, not because of the technical problems but because of the cost, the unpopularity of arms manufacture, and the ease with which so-called alternatives could be presented to the public.

Fortunately, behind all the chopping and changing in the White House and Pentagon lay some real strength in the B-52 force of SAC, although even this has dramatically shrunk and suffered many severe difficulties. The B-52 was the first truly strategic jet aircraft, and it was made possible by the development of the J57 turbojet by Pratt & Whitney which offered not only high power but also reduced fuel consumption. By using no fewer than eight of these

engines (which at first, in 1950, had a thrust of 4 tonnes each) Boeing was able to build a bomber that could fly a round-trip mission between US bases and any likely targets. The first flight took place in April 1952, and by 1955 a considerably modified B-52A, with a new nose with a side-by-side cockpit, was in squadron service with SAC. A few months later three flew round the world non-stop, with several air refuellings.

Eventually 744 of these giant bombers were built, in eight successive versions. Each introduced significant improvements, which culminated in the B-52G and H. The former brought in sealed 'integral tank' wings housing much more fuel than previously, as well as a shorter fin and a remotely controlled tail turret, the gunner now sitting up front with the five other crew. In the B-52H of 1961 the J57 engines (in most B-52 versions increased in power to 6237 kg/ 13,750 lb) were replaced by a new engine derived from the J57, the TF33 turbofan, of 7771 kg (17,000 lb) thrust combined with dramatically reduced fuel consumption and noise. Despite its weight of 229 tonnes, compared with 177 for the prototype, the B-52H gets off the ground faster and has a much better all-round

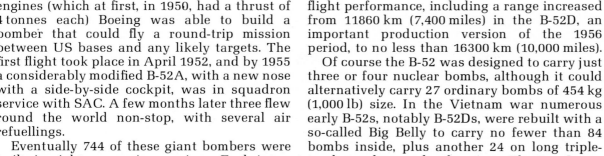

flight performance, including a range increased from 11860 km (7,400 miles) in the B-52D, an important production version of the 1956 period, to no less than 16300 km (10,000 miles).

Of course the B-52 was designed to carry just three or four nuclear bombs, although it could alternatively carry 27 ordinary bombs of 454 kg (1,000 lb) size. In the Vietnam war numerous early B-52s, notably B-52Ds, were rebuilt with a so-called Big Belly to carry no fewer than 84 bombs inside, plus another 24 on long triple-tandem pylons under the wings. The B-52G was built to carry eight nuclear bombs internally and two Hound Dog cruise missiles on underwing pylons, but the Hound Dog was withdrawn in 1976. In its place the B-52G, which with 193 built was the most numerous B-52 version, today carries up to 12 supersonic SRAMs (short-range attack missiles), each of which can fly by itself to a target more than 160 km (100 miles) away from the point of release. A further eight SRAMs can be loaded on a rotary launcher in the internal weapon bay. The same total of 20 SRAMs can be carried by the B-52H, of which 102 were built, and these two advanced models of the B-52, the G and H, have also been progressively updated with several extremely comprehensive and costly structural and avionics (aviation electronics) modifications to keep them competitive.

The most important recent additions to the B-52s have been a completely new OAS (offensive avionics system) costing $1,662 million to help these large, aged and conspicuous aircraft to penetrate hostile airspace, and the ALCM (air-launched cruise missile). Originally the ALCM, the Boeing AGM-86B, was interchangeable with SRAM and thus carried on the internal launcher as well as the wing pylons. Now it has been lengthened to hold more fuel and fly further, over 2400 km (1,500 miles), so although 12 can be carried externally none can be carried internally until the bomb bays have been rebuilt. The first 16 B-52Gs with cruise missiles became operational in December 1982. Under the terms of the SALT 2 agreement they have extra pieces called strakes fixed to the wings which the Russians can see from satellites.

As the B-52 cannot quite go on for ever SAC was forced to buy 76 small swing-wing FB-111A bombers in 1967, and these began to equip two wings of 30 aircraft each from 1971. The FB-111A can carry two SRAMs or nuclear bombs internally and four more SRAMs on underwing pylons, but its range is inadequate for true strategic use despite air refuelling. The gigantic stainless-steel six-engined XB-70 Valkyrie, able to cruise at Mach 3 (3200 km/h or 2,000 mph), was never put into production. Instead ten years of detailed studies led to a 1970 contract for the Rockwell B-1 bomber, with new GE F101 augmented turbofan engines in the 14-tonne thrust class. The first of four prototypes of this impressive swing-wing four-seat bomber flew on 23 December 1974, and flight trials were extremely successful. Though not far short of the B-52 in size, and much greater in capability, the

B-1 had a radar signature (appearance on enemy radar displays) less than one-tenth that of a B-52, and it was specially designed to penetrate enemy territory at the lowest possible level. On board are the most comprehensive defensive and offensive avionics put into a bomber.

In July 1977 the B-1 was cancelled by President Carter, but this could not stop the need becoming even more urgent. After much argument President Reagan announced in September 1981 that the USAF would at last get 100 of a developed version, the B-1B, between 1986 and 1988. Features of the B-1B are much greater fuel tankage to give a range of over 11300 km (7,000 miles), fixed engine inlets, extraordinarily comprehensive and advanced avionics, special provision for rapid start-up and fast take-off to escape missile attack, and the ability to carry 38 nuclear bombs, 22 ALCMs, 38 SRAMs or 36288 kg (80,000 lb) of ordinary bombs (84 bombs internally plus 44 externally). The existing wing sweep of the B-1 will be simplified for the B1-B as the aircraft will always enter enemy radar space at low level and at subsonic speeds.

Britain's splendid Vulcan tailless-delta bombers had almost vanished from the RAF when the Falklands conflict brought them back into the limelight. Some were hastily equipped with 21 bombs while others were converted as tankers with a hosereel in the tail replacing the main ECM (electronic countermeasures, a major defensive avionic system intended to interfere with enemy radar systems) installation. Bombing raids flown from Wideawake airfield on Ascension Island against the runway at Port Stanley involved an amazing 12800 km (8,000-mile) round-trip, by far the longest in the history of air warfare. The main tankers used to make these missions possible were Handley Page Victor K.2s, which themselves were converted from one-time strategic bombers.

China uses H-6 bombers (Tu-16 'Badgers' made at Xian) with freefall nuclear or conventional bombs. The only other strategic air power is France, whose Dassault Mirage 4A bombers are in the same class as the FB-111A, able to fly at Mach 2 at high altitude but in practice confined to subsonic attacks at treetop heights over relatively short ranges. C-135F tankers are used for probe/drogue inflight refuelling (where the receiver aircraft inserts a probe into a funnel carried by the tanker), and pairs of Mirage 4As can take off with one acting as a tanker to top up its partner, but even so it is hard-pressed to fly to a target 1000 km (620 miles) away at low level and return. The Mirage 4A is much larger than the Mirage fighters, and has two 7000 kg (15,430 lb) Atar 9K afterburning turbojets. It can carry over 7 tonnes of bombs, but the usual load would be a single 60-kilotonne nuclear bomb. By 1989 the ASMP (*air/surface moyenne portée*, or air-surface long range) missile may be in use, probably carried in pairs under the wings, although these aircraft may be withdrawn before that year. A total of 33 is available for combat missions in 1983.

Twelve Mirage 4As were converted as reconnaissance aircraft, and this remains a vital role for the strategic aircraft. Some of the most

BELOW No aircraft has ever been the subject of so many studies and delays as the US Air Force B-1. In the mid-1960s its original version, AMSA (Advanced Manned Strategic Aircraft), was said to mean 'America's Most Studied Airplane'. The first B-1 flew in 1974, but none will reach a USAF squadron until 1985, nor become ready for operations until August 1986.

Rockwell International B-1B
Country of origin: USA.
Dimensions and weights: Wingspan, 15°: 41·67 m (136 ft 8½ in), 67·5°: 23·84 m (78 ft 2½ in); length 44·81 m (147 ft 0 in); maximum loaded weight 216365 kg (477,000 lb).
Engines: Four 13608 kg (30,000 lb) thrust class GE F101-102 augmented turbofans.
Max. speed: Low-level, 1000 km/h (621 mph).
Range: More than 12000 km (7,455 miles).
Military load: Internal bays for 84 bombs of 227 kg (500 lb) or up to 24 nuclear bombs or 8 AGM-86 B/C or 24 SRAM missiles, plus various external loads.

extraordinary aircraft in the sky are modified Boeing KC-135 tankers or C-135 transports equipped for various kinds of electronic or other reconnaissance, often with grotesque bulges, blisters, probes, trailing wires or rows of blade aerials (antennae). Another aircraft of the same family is the larger E-3A Sentry Awacs (Airborne Warning and Control System) which carries a giant radar with a rotating aerial on a pylon above the fuselage. Britain's counterpart, the Nimrod AEW.3, has a better arrangement with an aerial at each end of the fuselage. One covers 180° ahead and the other the 180° sector astern without any parts of the aircraft itself getting in the way. Largest and most powerful current military aircraft are the E-4B command posts, based on the Boeing 747, which in any crisis would form the seat of the US government and national military command.

In the mid-1950s Lockheed built the U-2 as a kind of ultra-high-flying jet sailplane to carry out clandestine reconnaissance (until one was shot down by Soviet SAM defences on 1 May 1960). Next came the amazing Lockheed SR-71 'Blackbird', able to fly faster than any other military aircraft; one holds the world speed record at 3530 km/h (2,200 mph). SR-71s equip the 9th Strategic Reconnaissance Wing of SAC, and have flown remarkable missions in many parts of the world; one flew from New York to London in only 1 hour 55 minutes. Today not even extreme speed and height can prevent interception. In 1982 the USAF began taking delivery of TR-1 reconnaissance aircraft derived from the subsonic U-2, and relying entirely on clever avionics for some kind of protection. But the word that is on the lips of many aircraft designers today is 'stealth'.

Stealth technology means the measures taken to try to keep an aircraft invisible to defending radars, or, if that is not possible, to cause such confusion that defences cannot get their SAMs and interceptor fighters to pinpoint its position and shoot it down. Stealth techniques are highly classified (secret), but they involve careful shaping of the exterior of the aircraft, avoiding flat surfaces and angles or corners that could act as radio-wave reflectors, and the installation of jet engines either on top of the aircraft or hidden inside at the downstream end of long curved inlet ducts, the use of RAM (radar absorbent materials) added on top of the outer skin, and all the available avionic systems and decoys (such as chaff, jammers and flares) to throw defending radars and missiles off the scent.

Designers have tried for a long time to reduce the radar signature of their bombers, but it is only in the past five years that real breakthroughs have been made. Already, thanks to careful shaping, modified engine ducts and widespread use of RAM coatings, the big B-1B will have a radar signature much less than that of the B-1 prototypes; indeed it has been said that the signature will be only one-hundredth of a B-52. Much further work is now going ahead in the USA – and, unquestionably, in the Soviet Union – to try and develop completely stealth-designed bombers for the final decade of this century.

In recent years, numerous American artists have shown possible shapes for such aircraft, but these are unlikely to be very close to whatever may prove to be the next generation of strategic aircraft beyond the B-1B and 'Blackjack'. The one thing that can be predicted with certainty is that they will be unlike anything seen before, because no aircraft have to meet such a challenging environment.

ABOVE *Seen here with its eight landing wheels extended on return from a mission, the SR-71 is the fastest-ever military aircraft, with a speed of over 3500 km/h (2,180 mph). They are painted a dull bluish-black to radiate heat, but at full speed the nozzles of the two engines glow bright red.*

FIGHTERS

PRECEDING PAGES *When Dassault designed the Mirage F1 the company never expected that it would later go back to the tailless delta, although in a very different new-technology form. Outwardly today's Mirage 2000 resembles older Mirage IIIs, but in fact it is wholly new.*

BELOW *In the mid-1960s the British government cancelled all the new British warplanes then under development and bought American replacements. Both the RAF and Royal Navy received F-4 Phantom fighters which, at great cost, were redesigned to have Rolls-Royce engines (but instead of making them faster the more powerful engines caused so much extra drag that the British Phantoms are actually slower). This Phantom FGR.2 (FGR means fighter, ground attack and reconnaissance) flies with RAF No 29 Sqn. Today it is painted all grey and is in the Falkland Islands.*

By definition, a fighter is an aircraft intended to shoot down other aircraft. For some 70 years they have been relatively powerful yet small aircraft with the greatest possible agility and a rapid and steep climb to get up quickly to high-flying enemies. Almost all fighters have had fixed guns or rockets firing ahead, and so the pilot or an automatic control system has brought the armament to bear by aiming the whole aircraft using the normal flight controls.

A few fighters in World War 2 had power-driven gun turrets, but these were not a success. In the 1950s several Soviet fighters had guns in the nose which could be pivoted up or down, and today the General Dynamics corporation is studying an F-16 with a gun which can be aimed over a modest arc of fire independently of the aircraft (this is just one example among many current study programmes). Not least, the advent of the long-range guided AAM (air-to-air missile) removed some of the pressure from fighter designers and left it to the missile to effect the final deadly closure and kill. In fact, in 1959 the US Navy almost bought the Douglas F6D Missileer which was a carrier-based aircraft of quite low speed and modest manoeuvrability. Its function was to loiter near the Fleet with a deadly load of six large Eagle AAMs, each of which could destroy enemy aircraft from distances up to 200 km (125 miles). Thus the F6D was merely an aerial launch platform, and not at all the kind of aircraft normally associated with the word fighter.

In World War 2 fighters were divided into the small single-seaters, the large two-seater long-range escorts (which soon proved unable to hold their own in combat) and radar-equipped night fighters. The latter remained a separate class until quite recently when progressive reduction in the size and weight of radars at last made it possible for all fighters to operate with equal effectiveness in all conditions of night or bad weather. Today it is inconceivable that anyone would design a fighter not equipped with all-weather avionics, but fighters are still to some extent divided into long-range interceptors (often with two engines, two crew and very powerful radar and long-range missiles) and short-range dogfighters in which other variables are sacrificed for the ultimate in manoeuvrability and flight performance.

There is also very close kinship between most fighters and attack aircraft. Many aircraft exist in both attack and fighter forms (the Viggen, Harrier, Tornado, Mirage 2000, F-15, MiG-23/27 and F-104 are obvious examples) while the F-111 is an example of a fighter that became a pure attack aircraft and the F-4 an attack aircraft that became a fighter. As originally planned in the mid-1950s the F-4 had 11 stores pylons and was to be a powerful Marine Corps attack machine. Late in design it was recast as a Fleet defence fighter; ten of the pylons were removed, leaving just one on the centreline for a tank, and four Sparrow radar-guided missiles were recessed under its broad belly. At that time, 1957, guns

were widely thought to be obsolete, and the F-4 entered US Navy service in 1960–61 as the most powerful and highest-performing fighter in the world.

It was so good it was evaluated by the USAF, which bought it in very large numbers not only as a fighter but also as an attack aircraft, designated F-4C, carrying the unprecedented bombload of 7258 kg (16,000 lb). The next USAF version, the F-4D, was specially equipped as an attack machine, with both nuclear and conventional bombs, rockets and ASMs (air-to-surface missiles) while retaining its original capability as a fighter. Then in Vietnam close dogfights with agile cannon-armed Communist MiGs showed that the F-4 had severe deficiencies, and the F-4E went into production with a slatted wing and an internal gun. Since then no major new fighter has omitted to carry a gun.

One of the few aircraft to rival the F-4 for speed is the F-104 Starfighter, and this was designed by Lockheed on the basis of experience in the Korean war (1950–53). Pilots in that conflict cried out for performance at all costs, and the F-104 was made to fly at over Mach 2, one of its features being the smallest and thinnest wing ever flown on a fighter. So low is the F-104's drag that it achieves this performance on just one engine identical to the two used in the F-4; but the small wing gravely limited its value as a fighter (because of poor manoeuvrability, especially when at the slowish 700 km/h/435 mph speeds typical of close

combat) and also as an attack machine (because there was hardly anywhere to hang bombs). By 1960 Lockheed had designed a stronger, heavier and much more complex version, the F-104G, chiefly to carry nuclear weapons at very high speed at low level, and also to fly tactical reconnaissance missions with internal or external cameras. But right at the end of its development the Italians chose the F-104 as an interceptor, so the wheel turned full circle with the F-104S which has a radar designed primarily for the air-to-air role and armament of a gun, medium-range Sparrow AAMs (or Italy's own Aspide, which is very similar) and close-range Sidewinder AAMs. Nobody could pretend the F-104 is ideal because its turning circle is large and it could never hold its own against a modern fighter such as an F-16, but the F-104S does offer considerable defensive capability against likely enemy aircraft for a modest financial outlay.

Somewhat in the same class in being relatively small and light and having a modest-sized wing, the Northrop F-5 has been developed through three distinct generations of fighters which, despite very limited interest by their home customers in the USA, have sold by the thousand to air forces all over the world. The original F-5A Freedom Fighter was powered by two tiny GE J85 turbojets, each rated at 1850 kg (4,080 lb) with full afterburner, and was armed with two guns and two Sidewinder AAMs. First flown in July 1959, and as a production aircraft in May 1963, the F-5A was sold in 16 countries

ABOVE *The Lockheed F-104 Starfighter was designed in 1952–4 as an air-combat fighter, notable for its amazingly small and thin wings. By 1960 the F-104G was being built in large numbers for export customers mainly as an attack bomber. In the late 1960s Italy developed this final version, the F-104S, as an all-weather interceptor. Thus the wheel turned full circle and the newest F-104s are fighters.*

and more than 1,000 (including the F-5B two-seater and RF-5 reconnaissance version) were sold in ten years. In November 1970 the slightly improved F-5E Tiger II emerged winner of an IFA (International Fighter Aircraft) competition and proved even more successful, despite again failing to be adopted as a regular type for the inventory of any of the US services (although it was adopted as an economic demonstrator of close combat techniques by USAF and Navy 'Top Gun' *Aggressor* squadrons which train fighter pilots, and on occasion F-5Es simulate Soviet MiG-21s and other possible enemies). Inevitably the F-5E has radar, and as well as retaining two Sidewinders on the wingtips and two 20 mm guns in the nose it can carry 3175 kg (7,000 lb) of stores on five pylons. Together with the two-seat F-5F more than 1,300 had been ordered by late 1982, which is a much higher total than any single modern non-US or Soviet fighter adopted by its own air force.

Availability of a much more powerful GE engine, the F404 augmented turbofan of 7433 kg (16,387 lb) thrust, opened the way to the ideal third-generation F-5, the F-20A Tigershark. (An augmented turbofan has an afterburner in which extra fuel can be burned to give more thrust.) First flown in August 1982, this single-engined machine has roughly twice the power of its twin-engined predecessors and thus a flight performance and manoeuvrability rivalling that of its much more expensive competitors. A modern coherent-pulse-doppler radar (the type of radar needed to meet today's demands to look down and fire on aircraft skimming the surface) is combined with numerous other updates and there seems no doubt that the F-20 will reach a four-figure sales total like its two preceding generations.

One of the first and best attempts to build a really small jet fighter, and thus gain in agility and dogfight performance while also slashing costs, was the British Folland Gnat of 1954. This was scorned by the RAF, but despite this its obvious qualities were so attractive it actually found a few foreign sales, and in India large numbers were made under licence and, armed with two 30 mm Aden cannon, did very well

these superbly finished machines impressed their recipients by their tough reliability, excellent manoeuvrability and devastating punch from two/three 30 mm guns firing ammunition roughly twice as powerful as that of British or French guns of the same calibre.

In contrast the Soviet Union quickly dropped the MiG-19 in favour of its successor, the MiG-21. In the immediate post-Korean period Soviet aerodynamicists decided there were two best shapes for future supersonic fighters, one with a 62° swept wing and the other with a 55° delta (triangular) wing, in both cases with flaps fitted and conventional horizontal tail. The swept shape, already used for the MiG-19, was adopted by Sukhoi for an attack aircraft, but the MiGs of this family remained prototypes. In contrast the tailed deltas went into quantity production to the designs of both bureaux. The MiG-21 became one of the most prolific fighters of all time, with about 12,000 built in more than 30 versions. Early models were extremely simple and carried little but one or two guns, two dogfight AAMs similar to the Sidewinder and a gunsight. With each new version the MiG-21 became more capable, with greater power, more fuel, more weapons and more avionics, and a few were still being made in 1982 with the top of the fuselage bulged from cockpit to tail, and with overall performance still adequate to be useful (although not in the same class as the fighters of 1970 or later basic design). Sukhoi's deltas were bigger, and from the start equipped with radar and AAMs for use as interceptors. The Su-9 soon gave way to the Su-11 with more power and later radar and missiles; this in turn was replaced by the extremely fast Su-15 twinjet of which about 1,000 were delivered in 1969–76. Called 'Flagon' by NATO, the Su-15 is still a leading Soviet interceptor, armed with a pair of large missiles.

In the mid-1950s two other European nations built delta fighters, but these were both tailless. Sweden's J35 Draken was the most advanced

against larger and less-nimble opponents such as the F-86 and F-104. By 1976 India's Hindustan Aeronautics had begun production of a developed Gnat named Ajeet (Invincible) with integral-tank wings which allow the pylons to be used for weapons instead of drop tanks. Almost 100 had been made by 1983, including a purely Indian tandem trainer version quite unlike the British Gnat Trainer.

Developing practical supersonic fighters for the first time was a difficult task, but the two pioneers were both famous. The USAF's North American (now Rockwell) F-100 Super Sabre had almost vanished by the 1980s except in Turkey, but the Soviet MiG-19 continues to be a very important type thanks to the Chinese who recognized that, far from being obsolete by the 1960s, it was one of the best fighters of all in close visual combat. China never showed much interest in the radar-equipped interceptor version with AAM armament, but instead built the basic MiG-19 day fighter in large numbers, calling it the J-6. Several thousand were made, including hundreds exported at low prices, and fighter concept in the world when it began in 1950, and eventually 606 were built in eight main versions. More than in any other fighter the design team packaged everything from front to rear, which among other things resulted in the inner wing having the amazing leading-edge sweep of 80°! The outer wing was more normal, giving what was called a double-delta configuration. All models were powered by a locally made Rolls-Royce Avon jet with Swedish afterburner, and the early 30 mm gun armament gave way to various AAMs homing by IR (infra-red, heat) and radar methods. IR and radar homing guidance each have their own advantages, and it is significant that Soviet interceptors normally carry at least one missile of each type to ensure best performance under all conditions. In the West no attempt has been made to offer both systems to pilots; the radar version of Sidewinder was withdrawn, and the medium-range Sparrow has never had IR guidance.

The other European delta was the French Dassault Mirage. Intensely nationalistic, the Dassault company had no idea of the fantastic success the Mirage would enjoy, largely because of the absence of commercial rivals. Powered by an improved version of the 1946-vintage Atar turbojet, rated at 6000 kg (13,230 lb) thrust with afterburner, the original Mirage III entered service in 1960 as a simple Mach 2 interceptor

with a missile and two cannon (an alternative to the latter was a booster rocket engine) and extremely high all-round performance. It was also intended to fly attack missions (although at first Marcel Dassault himself objected to bombs spoiling the look of his most beautiful creation) and also operate from rough and short front-line airstrips, but as tailless deltas of this kind take off and land at extremely high speeds in excess of 300 km/h (190 mph) the small airstrip claim was curious. In fact, almost all the Mirage III, 5 and 50 fighters sold around the world have operated from the best runways available; indeed in many air forces that use the Mirage there are no other suitable runways in the country, so dispersal to avoid enemy attack is impossible.

Dassault's Mirage hit world headlines when Israeli Mirage IIICJ fighters routed opposition from several Arab air forces in the 1967 war. Even before this time Dassault had sold many versions with single- or two-seat cockpits, various weapons and radar fits and special camera noses for reconnaissance. From 1964 efforts had been made to find a successor, and after abortive development of much larger Mirages with delta wings, high-mounted conventional wings and lift-jets giving V/STOL (vertical/short take-off and landing) it was decided to build a small version of the tailed high-wing machine,

BELOW The Soviet MiG-21 has been built in greater numbers than any other combat aircraft since 1945, and probably exported to more countries (at least 37). All of the numerous versions have a delta (triangular) wing and separate horizontal tail. This MiG-21RF is a camera-packed reconnaissance model used by Egypt, armed here with AA-2-2 'Advanced Atoll' missiles.

Mikoyan/Guryevich MiG-21PFMA (R is sub-variant of this)
Country of origin: Soviet Union.
Dimensions and weights: Wingspan 7·15 m (23 ft 5½ in); length 15·76 m (51 ft 8½ in); maximum loaded weight 9400 kg (20,725 lb).
Engine: One 6200 kg (13,668 lb) Tumanskii R-11F2S-300 augmented turbojet.
Maximum speed: 2150 km/h (1,335 mph).
Range: Ferry range, 1800 km (1,118 miles).
Military load: One 23 mm gun with 200 rounds plus up to 2000 kg (4,409 lb) external stores including two/four AA-2-2 'Advanced Atoll' or AA-8 'Aphid' AAMs.

matched to a single Atar engine. The result was the Mirage F1, flown in 1966, and despite having a much smaller wing than the deltas this wing is so much more effective that it can carry much greater weights of fuel and weapons and yet land slower and use smaller airstrips. The F1 family are excellent aircraft of which some 700 were ordered, with deliveries nearing 600 by 1983. The family includes fighter, day attack (no radar), dual trainer and multi-sensor reconnaissance versions, and South Africa has a construction licence as well as numerous French-supplied F1s supplementing the earlier Mirage III deltas.

Many people were surprised when, after again making abortive sorties into the field of large Mirages with swing-wings (often with two engines) and an officially sponsored ACF (*Avion de Combat Futur*), Dassault returned to the baby tailless delta formula with the Mirage 2000, first flown in March 1978. In fact, the Mirage 2000 is far more advanced than its delta predecessors, and it is the first aircraft in Western Europe (but not in the world) built to what is called CCV (Control-Configured Vehicle) technology. Thanks to the perfection of electronically signalled flight-control systems, which can apply precise control demands with lightning speed, it is possible to build aircraft that are unstable, almost in the way a dart would be if its flights were on the point instead of at the tail. This enables the aircraft to be much more agile in combat, and it also reduces drag by eliminating the need (present in all ordinary aircraft) for the tail or wing trailing-edge elevons to keep pushing downwards to cancel out a nose-down lack

of balance in normal flight. The CCV fighter can be perfectly balanced in fore-and-aft trim, yet because of its basic instability turn with amazing suddenness in any direction under the computerized command of its power-driven control surfaces.

The Mirage 2000 does not look particularly different from the original Mirage III, but not only does it have all the CCV advantages but also its broad wings (larger than in earlier models) have power-driven hinged surfaces along the leading edge as well as the trailing edge, in order to take off and land more slowly and make much tighter turns in combat. Like most modern fighters part of the airframe of the Mirage 2000 is made of carbon-fibre composite material, which is much stronger than steel yet much lighter than aluminium. Another feature is

ABOVE *In 1963 Dassault began the study of successors to the delta-winged Mirage III and by 1966 had flown the more conventional Mirage F1, with a high-mounted wing and separate tailplane. An excellent fighter, the F1 is superior to the Mirage III and 5 in every respect. This is an F1.C of GC 1/5 squadron of l'Armée de l'Air (French air force).*

that the thin wing is blended in a curve into the body, which increases strength, reduces weight and aerodynamic drag and makes more space available for avionics or fuel. Armament remains two 30 mm guns and AAMs, but the latter are much better than the missiles of the earlier Mirage deltas (the same AAMs, the Super 530 and Magic, are carried by the Mirage F1).

Back in the 1960s Dassault had investigated the possible improvement in take-off, landing and turn radius that could be achieved by adding small canard (tail-first) surfaces on the nose. They were made retractable, and when extended were called moustaches. They were not adopted, but when the Israelis decided to build their own improved version of the Mirage III, using the shorter and more powerful American J79 engine, they finally added large canard foreplanes on the engine inlet ducts, with a significant improvement in turn radius, load carrying and low-speed handling. Technically, this Israeli fighter, the Kfir, could not rival the

basically newer Mirage 2000 but it was far better than the older Mirages and, had it not been for US embargoes imposed because of the use of an American engine, the Kfir would have achieved wider export sales. Price comparisons are seldom meaningful, but on published figures a 1982 customer could have from five to seven Kfirs for a single Mirage 2000.

In the Mirage 2000 there are no moustache foreplanes, although there are small strakes on the inlets in the same place as the Kfir's foreplanes. But in the bigger twin-engined Mirage 4000 there are large canard foreplanes, as in the Kfir, but with the added feature of being pivoted and power-driven as a primary control in the pitching plane. The Mirage 4000 is a unique, and scarcely believable, example of a modern combat aircraft built as a private venture, with no customer. While in the Tornado programme three major nations have struggled to build a warplane ordered in large numbers, Dassault has alone paid for the development

price of the 4000 would be extremely unattractive, especially in comparison with such alternatives as the F-15 (far more powerful and highly developed) and F-18. Despite the astronomic price Dassault has already sold the Mirage 2000 to India and Egypt and both may even build it under licence. An attack version is being developed, with different radar and multiple weapon pylons, but large-area delta wings are highly unsuited to the low-level attack mission which calls instead for the smallest wings possible.

For the long-range stand-off interceptor the wings are relatively unimportant. All that is needed is enough lift to get the heavy aircraft off

Dassault-Breguet Mirage F1.C
Country of origin: France.
Dimensions and weights: Wingspan
8.4 m (27 ft 6¾ in); length 15.0 m (49 ft 2½ in);
max. weight 16200 kg (35,715 lb).
Engine: One 7200 kg (15,873 lb) SNECMA
Atar 9K-50 augmented turbojet.
Maximum speed: Clean, high altitude,
2337 km/h (1,452 mph).
Range: Not published.
Military load: Two 30 mm guns, plus up to
4000 kg (8,820 lb) of external stores including
Matra Super 530 and 550 Magic AAMs.

---

of an aircraft that is even bigger and more powerful than the Tornado in the mere hope that a customer will emerge! Though a superb CCV-type flying machine, powered by two M53 engines similar to that of the Mirage 2000, the Mirage 4000 offers only marginally greater capability than the 2000 and in close combat is almost certainly inferior. As even the small Mirage 2000 is priced at $39 to $50 million, the

a long well-surfaced runway; there is no need to use frontline strips or bother about manoeuvrability in combat. Thus, in theory an interceptor could be a version of an attack aircraft, with the same high wing-loading. One of the largest fighters in the world, the Soviet Tu-128 'Fiddler' was derived from the Tu-28 attack aircraft, and probably has no capability in close air combat at all. Its objective was to destroy Western bombers before they could launch stand-off missiles such as Hound Dog or Blue Steel, and the great range (1500 km/930-mile radius) this demanded resulted in a fighter 27 metres (90 feet) long and weighing 45 tonnes. The Tu-128 carries a very large and powerful radar and two pairs of big AAMs (called AA-5 'Ash' by NATO) on wing pylons, one pair having IR guidance and the other semi-active radar. This big machine can reach Mach 1.75 and carries pilot and radar operator in tandem cockpits, but as it was designed more than 20 years ago its radar is unable to detect aircraft penetrating at treetop

ABOVE *When in 1967 France refused to deliver a large batch of Mirage 5s to Israel, even though they had been paid for, Israel decided to build its own fighters. This is a Kfir (Lion Cub) C2, originally based on the Mirage 5 but greatly altered with an Israeli-built General Electric J79 engine and almost totally Israeli avionics.*

height. There has been speculation in the West about how far the Tu-128 has been updated, and in 1982 it was said it was being replaced by an interceptor version of the Tu-22 bomber. The more likely replacements would be the Su-27, a completely new and seemingly outstanding twin-jet in the class of a modern F-14, and the latest version of MiG-25.

The MiG-25 is the fastest fighter of all time, because it was designed in 1958–62 to intercept the 3200 km/h (2,000 mph) B-70 bomber. The American B-70 was cancelled but the MiG-25 went ahead, and was first seen at an airshow in 1967. It was the first of a new breed of fighter with an extremely broad box-like body housing enormous inlet ducts to side-by-side engines of large diameter, a thin nose projecting ahead of the inlets, an almost unswept wing and twin canted vertical tails. It needed only a glance to see that the MiG-25 was planned as an ultra-fast stand-off killer, armed with powerful radar and large AAMs but having virtually no capability in close combat. When Western technicians inspected a MiG-25 that had been flown by a defecting pilot to Japan in 1976 they were surprised to find most of the structure made of steel, and titanium used only on a few leading edges and engine shrouds. The afterburning turbojets, each rated at 11 tonnes thrust, have water/methanol injection sprays to cool the air in the inlet ducts at speeds near the combat limit of Mach 2.8 (which is less than the limit attainable by the clean MiG-25 with pylons removed). Much of the technology was found to be typical of the time the MiG-25 was designed, the large radar of 600 kW output being packed with vacuum tubes (valves) instead of solid-state transistor technology, and using its power not so much for range as to burn through enemy

BELOW Fastest combat aircraft in the world, the Soviet MiG-25—known to NATO as 'Foxbat'—was first seen in 1967 and caused alarm in the West. Large and heavy, it is a stand-off interceptor and has no ability to manoeuvre in a dogfight. This Libyan example is carrying two giant AA-6 'Acrid' air-to-air missiles.

Mikoyan/Guryevich MiG-25
Country of origin: Soviet Union.
Dimensions and weights: Wingspan 13·95 m (45 ft 9 in); length 23·82 m (78 ft 1¾ in); maximum weight 36200 kg (79,800 lb).
Engines: Two 11000 kg (24,250 lb) Tumanskii R-31 augmented turbojets.
Maximum speed: Clean at high altitude 3400 km/h (2,113 mph).
Range: 2400 km (1,490 miles).
Military load: Normally two or four AAMs, such as one/two AA-6 'Acrid' with radar guidance and one/two AA-6 with IR guidance.

McDonnell Douglas F-15A/C Eagle
Country of origin: USA.
Dimensions and weights: Wingspan 13·05 m (42 ft 9¾ in); length 19·43 m (63 ft 9 in); maximum loaded weight 30845 kg (68,000 lb).
Engines: Two 10860 kg (23,940 lb) Pratt & Whitney F100-100 augmented turbofans.
Maximum speed: 2655 km/h (1,650 mph).
Range: With 'Fast pack' 5550 km (3,450 miles).
Military load: One 20 mm gun with 940 rounds, plus four AIM-7F or Amraam missiles plus four AIM-9 short-range missiles, or various air/surface weapons.

jamming. Most of the fuel is housed in double-skinned welded steel tanks of unusual form. Armament comprises four AAMs, either two IR and two radar 'Ash' or 'Anab' or, more often, two IR and two radar 'Acrid', the largest AAMs in use in the world. Over 400 MiG-25 interceptors serve in the Soviet PVO (air defence forces) and others are operating with Libya, Algeria and Syria. There are also reconnaissance and trainer versions, the former being used by India.

Existence of the MiG-25 triggered the development of a new fighter for the USAF. This was intended to be relatively small, agile and unbeatable in a dogfight, yet it eventually matured as one of the largest of all fighters, the mighty McDonnell Douglas F-15 Eagle, with an enormous high-mounted wing of 56.5 m² (608 ft²) area and several features − such as the wide boxy body with widely spaced inlet ducts and twin vertical tails − reminiscent of its Soviet predecessor. Pratt & Whitney produced a new augmented turbofan engine, the F100, the use of two conferring a ratio of thrust to weight which at low altitudes could handsomely exceed unity (so the F-15 can take off and climb vertically upwards, and indeed accelerate in a vertical climb to beyond Mach 1!). A 20 mm gun is mounted in the right wing root, four Sparrow radar-guided AAMs are carried nestled against the lower edges of the fuselage and close-range Sidewinders are hung on the inner wing pylons.

Hughes provided the APG-63 pulse-doppler radar for the F-15 which set new standards in power, versatility and in erasing everything from the cockpit display screen or HUD (head-up display, optically projected into the pilot's line of sight on the windscreen) except for information or targets of real value to the pilot. Thus the pilot at all times has a clear and uncluttered picture of the combat situation, and another new idea was the Hotas (hands on throttle and stick) formula in which, as far as possible, every control button or switch the pilot could ever need in combat was mounted either on the engine throttle levers or on the main control column handgrip.

By 1983 the USAF had bought 749 Eagles, later models being of the F-15C and two-seat F-15D type with programmable radars, greater tankage and provision for very large extra tanks, called Fast (fuel and sensor, tactical) packs, which conform to the sides of the fuselage and house an extra 4536 kg (10,000 lb) of fuel without increased drag. The F-15 already had the exceptional fuel capacity of 5260 kg (11,600 lb), not including the possible use of three drop tanks. With maximum fuel the gross weight can be well over 30 tonnes, double what

ABOVE The US Air Force's F-15 Eagle, built by McDonnell Douglas, was urgently designed in 1968–70 to counter the MiG-25, but today has been developed as a multi-role aircraft of great capability. Although slower than the MiG-25, it is far more useful, and carries many more kinds of weapon (but this example from the 36th Tactical Fighter Wing at Bitburg AB, Germany, is carrying only a single Sidewinder air-to-air missile).

the original concept had proposed but giving range for non-stop Atlantic crossing without use of tankers, a remarkable capability for a regular squadron fighter. Alternatively 7257 kg (16,000 lb) of external weapons can be carried, and since 1980 McDonnell Douglas has been developing a special all-weather interdiction version, the Strike Eagle, which can carry an external weapon load of 10885 kg (24,000 lb), approximately twice the bombload of any World War 2 heavy bomber and carried for much greater ranges. In 1983 this version had not yet been ordered by the USAF, partly because of the intense competition offered by

the F-16 from the General Dynamics corporation.

The F-16 began life as a mere LWF (Light Weight Fighter) demonstrator, to investigate what capability, if any, could be built into a fighter significantly smaller and lighter than the F-15, and thus costing considerably less. When the LWF programme was begun, in 1972, the cost of an F-15 – in the $15 million bracket – seemed extremely high and in the teeth of opposition from the USAF the Department of Defense pushed through the LWF without any real hope it would go into production. General Dynamics designed the Model 401 around a single F100 engine of the same type as the pair used in the F-15, fed through a plain inlet under the fuselage without the variable area or profile arrangement usually seen on supersonic inlets. The wing was given pivoted leading and trailing edges to adjust its camber to each flight condition, and the CCV concept, with electrically signalled controls, was taken to a more advanced level than in any previous aircraft. The pilot was put in a reclining seat under a completely transparent bubble canopy, with a near-perfect view in all directions, and his control column was a stubby handgrip on the right console along the cockpit wall, where the pilot could rest his arm, controlling the aircraft not by actually pivoting according to the pilot's

BELOW *The F-16 Fighting Falcon was originally just a demonstrator of light-fighter technology, but today it is the West's most important tactical aircraft, with 1,000 delivered to many nations and fantastic capability in many roles. This single-seat F-16A belongs to the KLu (Royal Netherlands air force).*

General Dynamics F-16A/C Fighting Falcon
Country of origin: USA.
Dimensions and weights: Wingspan (without wingtip missiles) 9·45 m (31 ft 0 in); length 15·09 m (49 ft 6 in); maximum loaded weight 16057 kg (35,400 lb).
Engine: One 10814 kg (23,840 lb) Pratt & Whitney F100-200 augmented turbofan.
Maximum speed: High altitude, clean, 2173 km/h (1,350 mph).
Range: Ferry range 3890 km (2,415 miles).
Military load: One 20 mm gun with 515 rounds, plus external loads up to ultimate limit of 9276 kg (20,450 lb).

hand movements like traditional control columns, but sensing the applied hand force without moving. Pilots found flying the Model 401 a new experience, and as the YF-16 it won over a Northrop rival, and by 1975 was developed into the F-16 Fighting Falcon, bought for the USAF.

In developing the YF-16 prototypes into the F-16, General Dynamics enlarged the aircraft slightly and built into it enormously enhanced capability, especially in the attack role. While strengthening the structure to have a service life of 8,000 hours despite repeatedly being subjected to the brutal acceleration of 9g in sustained turns – a force no other aircraft in the world is believed to have to endure on a repeated long-term basis – the F-16 has been made to carry an external weapon load of 6895 kg (15,200 lb), with a theoretical maximum load of 9276 kg (20,450 lb), an amazing figure for such a small aircraft and in fact in excess of the gross laden weight of the YF-16! A 20 mm gun is mounted in the left wing root, and a flight-refuelling receptacle is in the top of the fuselage (as it is in almost all US fighters). Sidewinder AAMs can be carried on the wingtips and other loads can include almost every tactical weapon in the NATO air forces.

In 1975 the F-16 was chosen to replace the F-104 by Belgium, Denmark, the Netherlands and

Norway and other customers include Israel, Egypt, South Korea and Pakistan. Israel was quick off the mark to use the immense capability of its new F-16s: on 7 June 1981 it sent eight, each with two 907 kg (2,000 lb) bombs, to demolish Iraq's Osirak nuclear station which had been suspected as a source of weapon-grade plutonium. Other F-16s dominated air fighting over the Lebanon in mid-1982, and incidentally gave a show of how to use chaff, flares and jammers to avoid hostile SAMs and AA artillery. By 1983 deliveries had passed the 1,000 mark, and the USAF – whose purchase of 1,388 to date, including 204 two-seaters, considerably exceeds that for the F-15 – is engaged in a long-term updating programme leading to the F-16C and two-seat F-16D which will have unequalled all-weather navigation and weapon-delivery systems.

General Dynamics has also flown two of the most technically interesting fighters ever built in the AFTI-16 and F-16XL (F-16E). The AFTI (Advanced Fighter Technology Integration) is a research aircraft fitted with an even more powerful flight-control system than the ordinary F-16, so that, together with modified control surfaces which include inclined canard foreplanes on the inlet duct, the pilot can do things never previously possible. He can make the AFTI move up, down, left or right instantly, without having to alter the attitude. Suppose he is making a firing run on a ground target and finds he is to the left of the desired flight path. An ordinary fighter has to be rolled to the right to turn on to the new sightline and then rolled to the left to line up on the target; the AFTI does not roll but with wings level merely zips the required distance to the right!

As for the F-16XL this is a considerably larger aircraft with a new cranked-arrow wing of enormous area, with trailing-edge elevons replacing the tailplane. It can carry twice the bombload of the ordinary F-16 for any given range – and get off the ground quicker – or fly twice as far with the same load. The first F-16XL, flown in mid-1982, was rebuilt from an F-16A, but the second has two seats and the powerful F110 engine which was also flown in a modified F-16A. Yet another F-16 had the old J79 engine, because of its much lower price and familiarity to export customers.

Great Britain, once a leader in fighter technology, suffered disastrously from the 1957 official view that fighters were obsolete. The Lightning interceptor was reluctantly allowed to continue, but proper development of it was stultified and there was no successor. Not until well into the 1970s was the RAF able to study a new British fighter and then a superb basic design already existed in the Panavia Tornado, initially configured as a multi-role all-weather attack and reconnaissance aircraft (as noted in the next chapter) but having large fuel capacity, extraordinarily economical and sophisticated augmented turbofan engines and a swing wing of advanced design able to match the conflicting requirements of short take-off at very high

ABOVE *The original Tornado (page 60) was developed as an attack aircraft, but the RAF needed a new long-range interceptor to guard the airspace from Iceland to the Baltic. The answer was a new Tornado version, now in production as the Tornado F.2, with a special radar and armed with Sky Flash missiles. It is shown with undercarriage doors closing after take off.*

weights, long range at subsonic speed and low-level attack at speeds faster than any other aircraft (1490 km/h/926 mph). It was natural for the RAF to use the Tornado as the basis for its new interceptor to patrol and defend the airspace from the Arctic to Gibraltar and from Iceland to the Baltic.

At first called Tornado ADV (air-defence variant) but now in production as the Tornado F.2, this version carries four Sky Flash AAMs – based on the radar-guided Sparrow but with an improved guidance system offering much greater lethality in the most adverse conditions – in two staggered tandem pairs recessed under the fuselage. Fitting in the long missiles required a slight lengthening of the fuselage, which in turn enabled 909 litres (200 gallons) of additional fuel to be accommodated internally.

The F.2's radar is completely new, the Marconi/Ferranti Foxhunter TWS (track-while-scan) pulse-doppler set which is considered in 1983 to be the best now in production for all-weather interception. The scanner is housed in a long pointed radome which, together with the longer body, gives slightly better acceleration and top speed without any change in engine. Only a single 27 mm gun is fitted instead of two, and other changes include new cockpit displays and controls, increased sweep and area of the fixed wing gloves (inboard of the outer-wing

pivots) and the provision of a neat retractable refuelling probe on the upper left side of the nose in place of a rather clumsy detachable probe on the right side. Sadly, to save money, the extremely formidable Sky Flash Mk 2 missile was cancelled, but late in the 1980s the American Amraam (Advanced medium-range AAM) may be fitted instead. In addition Sidewinder or, later, Asraam (Advanced short-range AAM) missiles can be carried on wing pylons, and it is almost certain that eventually this Tornado interceptor version will be required to fly attack missions as well, which would require merely small changes to the weapon control system and computer software (the programming giving the instructions to the automatic control systems).

Many other modern fighters also exist as attack aircraft, and one type, the F/A-18A Hornet described in the chapter on maritime aircraft, has been designed to be equally good at both sorts of mission. In Sweden the Draken was followed by the Saab-37 Viggen, again with a dramatic shape which in this case comprised a rear delta wing and a relatively large delta canard foreplane fitted like the main wing with trailing-edge flaps. Power is provided by a Swedish version of the American JT8D airline turbofan engine redesigned for flight at up to Mach 2. It is fitted with a Swedish afterburner and, for almost the first time on an afterburning engine, a reverser to help slow the aircraft after landing.

Unlike most air forces Sweden takes very seriously the need to disperse away from vulnerable fixed airfields, and one of the many challenging design requirements for the Viggen was the ability to operate from small rough airstrips and even from straight lengths of road in remote country areas where there is little traffic. This demands not only the ability to approach slowly under perfect control, but to land extremely accurately on strips less than one-third as wide as most runways and steer with precision on take-off or landing or when heading for a parking place among trees. The Viggen makes a no-flare landing, hitting the ground at its full rate of descent like a carrier-based aircraft, and then quickly thunders to a stop with its reverser in action and powerful non-skid brakes on its four small tandem mainwheels.

The first Viggens, in production in 1971, were of the AJ37 attack version, carrying heavy loads of external tanks, weapons and electronic gear. Then followed the SF37 and SH37 reconnaissance models, and the SK37 two-seat trainer, after which came the considerably altered JA37 interceptor with a modified engine, completely new pulse-doppler radar and weapon avionics, different flight controls (including the same taller kinked-tip fin as the trainer) and new weapons including a very powerful 30 mm gun under the body and a mix of Sky Flash and Sidewinder AAMs.

Saab is today working on the next-generation aircraft, the Model 2105 JAS (Swedish initials for fighter attack system). All Swedish fighters for many years have had to be equally good at a wide range of missions, and the JAS follows this tradition, and also has the laudable and tough objective of holding down cost. It would not be reasonable to expect it to be cheaper than the Viggen, even though it will be smaller, because inflation is everywhere making prices seem astronomical; but the JAS has been planned with exceptional care to offer the most economic defence to Sweden for the period 1990–2020. It will be a canard delta like the Viggen, but with a much slimmer body made possible by the choice

BELOW *In production since 1971 as an attack aircraft, Sweden's Saab 37 Viggen is now being produced as the JA37 interceptor. Although the only obvious distinguishing feature is the extended sweptback top to the fin (also a feature of the SK37 trainer), the JA37 has a revised engine and completely different radar and weapons.*

of a much more compact engine. The Tornado's RB.199 engine was almost ideal but – it is said on grounds of lower price – the American GE F404 was chosen, in a version fractionally more powerful than is fitted to the F/A-18A Hornet (but, unlike the Hornet, the JAS will be single-engined, which emphasizes the compact nature of this machine). The engine will be fed by simple fixed lateral inlets leaving the nose free for advanced radar and the wings and underside of the fuselage for a heavy load of AAMs and other ordnance. Great efforts are being made to design an avionic and cockpit system that will still be modern in the 1990s, and by early 1983 there was every indication that Sweden was well on the way to yet another extremely cost-effective combat aircraft developed entirely with Sweden's own budget and resources, although making maximum use of the best foreign technology in the US engine and British HUD (head-up display).

The only other aircraft in the same class being developed by one of the lesser powers is the IAI Lavi, of Israel. At first glance it seems ridiculous that the two nations should almost bankrupt themselves producing aircraft that are so nearly identical, but each has explained that collaboration is not possible. Israel is one of the most politically sensitive and threatened countries in the world, while Sweden is perhaps the most staunchly neutral. There is unfortunately no way the two could get together and build a common type, although whether each will actually succeed in putting its home-grown aircraft into service remains to be seen.

The Lavi (Lion Cub) again has an American engine, but in this case it is the Pratt & Whitney PW1120 augmented turbofan with maximum thrust rather greater than that of the F404 at 9344 kg (20,600 lb). It is fed by a chin inlet similar to that of the F-16, and while the wing has greater span than the JAS, and is mounted further to the rear, the canard foreplane is rather smaller and the fuselage shorter and more close-coupled. Clearly the Lavi is designed initially as a pure close-combat dogfighter, with maximum performance and agility, and with the attack mission's requirements not given quite the same overriding importance as in the case of the Swedish machine. Israel has published some clearly impossible timescales for the Lavi. A first flight might be possible in 1984–85, rather than the announced 1983, and several unofficial reports have suggested that the Lavi might soon become an international project with a technically powerful US partner (McDonnell Douglas has been tipped as the most likely).

Of course McDonnell Douglas has its own projects for advanced fighters, and for many years both the US Department of Defense and NASA (National Aeronautics and Space Administration) have funded major research programmes to find out how future fighters should best be designed. For example, Rockwell has built two HiMATs (Highly Manoeuvrable Aircraft Technology) under joint contract to the USAF and NASA to explore how future fighters can be given the greatest possible manoeuvrability. HiMAT is a pilotless RPV (remotely piloted vehicle), powered by a single J85 engine of the type used in the F-5 fighter. The configuration of the first is a tandem canard delta, with a swept rear wing and large swept canard foreplane above the ventral engine inlet. The wings have three sets of control surfaces as well as outward sloping wingtip fins; the foreplanes have acute dihedral (upward slope from root to tip on each side) and are fitted with elevators;

RIGHT *From February 1984 the Grumman X-29A FSW (forward-swept wing) demonstrator should confirm the calculated benefits of such a wing for future highly agile fighters. The recent development of advanced carbon fibre composite has made FSW structurally feasible. This photograph shows a model of the aircraft.*

and strong beams behind the main wing carry outward-sloping rudders. The first HiMAT flies at Mach 1.6 and can pull turns at a crushing 12g, under control from a pilot on the ground.

Another research aircraft is the Grumman X-29A, or FSW (forward-swept wing) demonstrator. There are several important advantages in a highly manoeuvrable fighter having a wing swept forward instead of to the rear, but until recently a high-speed FSW aircraft has been structurally impossible. This is because, just as the CCV idea makes the whole aircraft unstable, so does the FSW inevitably try to bend further and further under the aerodynamic loads, and the further it bends the greater is the load. The result would be that the wings would immediately break off, but today it is possible to make an FSW from advanced carbon fibre composite material that is so stiff it can stand up to the loads, even during violent manoeuvres. (A solid metal wing could have been made strong enough also, but its weight would have been prohibitive.) The X-29A is a small and supersonic machine powered by a GE F404 engine, and its flight programme from late 1983 was expected to show manoeuvrability and general handling superior to that of any previous supersonic aircraft.

Today it is possible the prize for fighter manoeuvrability may be held by the Soviet Union. For five years it has been known that the MiG design bureau has been producing prototypes of a new fighter, believed to have the service designation of MiG-29. Few firm details are yet known in the West, but it is thought to have features of the MiG-25 but on a smaller scale. Certainly it is a compact twin-jet with twin vertical tails, and according to some analysts who have good evidence its dogfight performance is extremely formidable. By 1982 a substantial number – certainly some dozens – of these agile machines were flying, and if past Soviet performance is any guide they will be tough, reliable and extremely good to fly. The previous MiG generation was a versatile swing-wing machine designated MiG-23 in its fighter role and MiG-27 in its attack version, and described in the next chapter. We do not yet know whether it is possible for the MiG-29 to fly both missions.

There is also the much larger Su-27 mentioned earlier, but we know so little about this that no discussion can be meaningful. What is rather disquieting is that these very advanced Soviet aircraft have been seen in numbers, whereas their counterparts in the West are mostly still on the drawing board. Nobody doubts Western ability. The ACA (Agile Combat Aircraft) proposed by British Aerospace, MBB of West Germany and Aeritalia is politically a marvellous achievement, because getting three major nations to agree on anything so emotive as a new fighter is intensely difficult. But do the nations have the money and the political will to translate a mock-up of 1982 into combat-ready squadrons in 1989?

ATTACK
AIRCRAFT

PRECEDING PAGES *No aircraft equals the Panavia Tornado in its combination of heavy weapon load, fuel-efficient engines, advanced avionics for precision navigation and weapon delivery, and swing wings for rock-steady flight at treetop height at 1450 km/h (901 mph). This Tornado is cruising at a lower speed and greater height, with its wings in an intermediate position.*

OPPOSITE TOP *The McDonnell Douglas A-4 Skyhawk was first flown in 1954 and remained in production 26 years. These A-4M Skyhawk IIs of the US Marine Corps have the 'camel hump' mentioned on this page.*

OPPOSITE BOTTOM *Although they look faintly like the MiG-21, the Sukhoi attack family are very much larger and more powerful. The original Su-7 of 1957 carried a small bombload and had a very short range, but was so strong and delightful to fly that it was well liked by its pilots. This is one of the much more capable swing-wing versions, an Su-17 of the Egyptian Air Force.*

Today the ground-attack aircraft occupies a central place among warplanes, but it was not always so. In World War 1 there were special armoured aircraft for attacking trenches, and in World War 2 most fighters were equipped to carry bombs, but throughout the Korean and Vietnam wars the US Air Force tended to fly its attack missions with fighters laden with ground-attack weapons. This was a major reason for many F-4 Phantoms stalling at low level and spinning into the ground, causing so many casualties that a new wing was devised with powerful leading-edge slats to help overcome the problem. Loading fighters with air-to-ground weapons is not always a good idea.

The first purpose-designed USAF attack aircraft in Vietnam was the Republic F-105. Nick-named the 'Thud', it was one of the most powerful and effective single-engined, single-seat aircraft ever built. It even had an internal bomb bay, but it is significant that this was generally used to house extra fuel, while the bombs were hung on external pylons. Thus, many modern attack aircraft – including the F-105 – look exactly like fighters. The popular media never recognize the category at all, and tend to stick to the traditional terms 'fighter' and 'bomber'. On this basis attack aircraft ought to be called bombers, because that is what they do, but the term somehow sounds derogatory. What makes it harder is that some attack aircraft, such as the Viggen and Tornado, have fighter versions, while some fighters, such as the F-15 and F-16, can carry heavy bombloads.

The first services to recognize the need for a purpose-designed attack category were the Soviet air force (the VVS) and the US Navy. The former was concerned only with land battles. For the past 50 years it has paid great attention to aircraft able to inflict severe losses on hostile armies, especially including armour, and this takes aircraft not only equipped with heavy guns and rockets or bombs but also well protected against ground fire. In contrast the US Navy is concerned with war at sea, and its attack aircraft are designed mainly for knocking out surface warships. This calls for equally good protection as well as special provisions for navigation, finding the enemy and accurate weapon delivery. Torpedoes are surprisingly little used, the main anti-ship weapons being missiles and bombs.

Perhaps the most successful attack aircraft of all time was the American Douglas A-4 Skyhawk, designed by Ed Heinemann in 1952 in a studied attempt to make combat aircraft smaller, simpler, cheaper, more reliable and easier to keep flying. To fly the missions called for, the US Navy calculated the aircraft would have to weigh 30,000 lb (13608 kg) loaded, but Heinemann's first A-4 in 1954 turned the scales at just half this! The wing was so small it did not need to fold, despite the A-4 being designed for use from carriers, and it not only had a full-span slat on each leading edge but it was sealed to form an integral fuel tank. The first A-4s had a British-designed J65 Sapphire jet of 3493 kg

(7,700 lb) thrust, but by 1962 the J52 had been substituted giving 4218 kg (9,300 lb) with better fuel efficiency. Extra avionics for navigation and weapon delivery were added behind the cockpit in what became called 'the camel hump' and production continued for a remarkable 26 years until the 2,980th was delivered in 1980. A prolonged production is the best way to keep down the price, and this is almost always achieved by the Soviet Union.

The West has problems with nationalistic feelings. In 1953 NATO launched a competition for a new light attack aircraft. It might not have been a formidable machine, for it was quite small and low powered, but it was specially designed to fly from small rough fields to avoid being destroyed in an attack on airfields (today all NATO airpower could be wiped out in seconds by nuclear missiles, but no action is taken). The winning design, first flown in 1956, was the Fiat (now Aeritalia) G91, but most countries refused to use it because their own design had not been selected. Only West Germany bought large numbers apart from the G91's native Italy. Today a few still fly in Portugal, while Italy uses the more formidable twin-engined G91Y.

What a contrast with a parallel Soviet programme, which began with the Sukhoi S-1 and S-2 prototypes of 1955. These were large single-engined machines in the class of the American F-105, but they suffered from having high fuel consumption and being unable to carry bombs *and* enough fuel for useful missions. Despite this, the type entered service as the Su-7 in 1958, and proved so beautiful to fly and so tough it remained in production for 25 years. Successive versions brought greater power, better rough-field capability (the Russians will never be knocked out on their airfields!) and eventually swing-wings giving twice the bombload for much greater ranges. The latest Su-22 versions have excellent nav/attack systems (shorthand for the avionics needed for all-weather navigation and attack) as well as devastating guns and heavy attack weapon loads, and because of the long production run their price remains amazingly low by Western standards.

One of the best of all Western attack aircraft is the British Aerospace (formerly Blackburn, then Hawker Siddeley) Buccaneer. Designed for the Royal Navy carrier force and first flown in 1958, it was one of the first aircraft specially engineered for attacking at very low level, to try to escape detection by enemy radars. It was thus made extremely strong, with very large internal fuel capacity (because jet engines burn fuel much faster at low altitudes) and with a large internal bomb bay, as well as two engines and two seats. High-pressure air piped from the engines is blown at supersonic speed from fine slits ahead of the wings, flaps, ailerons and tailplane, greatly increasing the effectiveness of these surfaces and allowing them to be made much smaller, which is of vital importance to low-level flight at high speed. Large-winged fighters cannot fly at full throttle at low level

without giving the pilot such a rough ride he may be unable to think clearly, and the structure may even be broken. With the elimination of the RN carriers the Buccaneers went to the RAF which had previously scorned them as slow and old fashioned. Only then did the RAF learn that with four 454 kg (1,000 lb) bombs in the weapon bay the Buccaneer can still attack at 1110 km/h (690 mph) which is faster than a Phantom or Mirage with the same load! Maximum bombload is no less than 7258 kg (16,000 lb), and the 'Bucc' has very long range as well. With standard fuel on a 'hi-lo-lo-hi' profile, it has an effective radius of almost 1000 km (620 miles); 'hi' stands for high altitude, where less fuel is burned, while 'lo' means the lowest possible safe height, seldom below 60 m (200 ft), to try and slide in 'under the enemy radar'. Thus most of the mission is covered as high as possible, while

49

ABOVE *In 1960 the West Germans picked an as yet unbuilt version of the Lockheed Starfighter (see F-104S, page 31), the F-104G, triggering off a chain reaction of sales to many other nations. A few are still in use. This F-104G of Germany's Marineflieger carries Kormoran anti-ship missiles.*

over defended territory the aircraft flies as 'lo' as possible.

Today all attack aircraft need help from ECM (electronic countermeasures) and if possible from special ECM aircraft. These help to analyse enemy radar and radio signals, and also warn of approaching hostile aircraft or missiles. Such systems even had to be installed in the Lockheed F-104G, which was derived from the F-104 fighter to carry nuclear weapons at low level and at about the speed of sound. In this attack role its very small wing is a great advantage. At quite the opposite end of the speed scale the Rockwell OV-10 Bronco and Argentinian Pucará are both twin-turboprops slower than World War 2 fighters and intended mainly for what are called 'brushfire' or limited small-scale wars. The Pucará was much in evidence in the Falklands campaign, one being brought to Britain for evaluation. Pucarás can carry plenty of weapons including cannon and machine guns and bombs of up to 1 tonne size, but are too vulnerable for modern battle areas.

The difficult task of the most advanced attack aircraft is called blind first-pass attack, in other words to make a high-speed attack on a small target without either having seen it or having to look for it. This demands the utmost precision in navigation and weapon delivery, and was beyond the capability of any aircraft until the General Dynamics F-111 entered service with the USAF in 1967. Designed in 1960–2 the F-111 was originally called a 'tactical fighter' and was meant to replace not only existing attack aircraft but also fighters. The USAF demanded such an enormous range that the F-111 came out extremely large, weighing as much as two loaded Flying Fortresses of World War 2. It never succeeded as a fighter, but became the West's most formidable attack aircraft (and one version, the FB-111A, has already been mentioned as a strategic bomber). One special attribute of the F-111 is its possession of a TFR under its nose. This device, a terrain-following radar, enables the aircraft automatically to follow the undulations of the ground while flying at full throttle only just above the surface. Nothing is more exciting, or terrifying, than making a TFR attack at night or in mist through mountains!

heavy bombload was made possible by leaving out most of the avionics. It was planned for Israel, where clear skies make visual attacks a common possibility, but amazingly was even bought by Belgium and many other countries where the weather is often bad and comprehensive nav/attack systems are essential.

Dassault also has a half-share in the far more useful Jaguar because it took over the former Breguet company which designed the Jaguar in partnership with BAC of Britain. Sadly Dassault has always competed against the Jaguar because it is half British, but despite this over 500 have been sold to five major customers. Powered by two fuel-efficient afterburning turbofans, the

Jaguar is an extremely effective aircraft with avionics for precision delivery and a bombload of over 4500 kg (9,900 lb) despite the fact it is one of the smallest of all modern combat aircraft. The RAF single-seat version has a self-contained inertial navigation system and a laser in the so-called chisel nose to give the exact distance of targets and to lock on to those 'marked' by a laser aimed by friendly troops on the ground. One of the most important attack weapons is the 'smart bomb' which steers itself automatically to any target illuminated with laser light. Thus, a hard-pressed soldier has only to point a small laser at an enemy tank or pillbox for it to be eliminated by a missile dropped by a friendly attack aircraft.

Japan's only modern combat aircraft is almost indistinguishable from the Jaguar, and uses the same engines made under licence in Japan. The Mitsubishi F-1 is actually a single-seat attack version of the T-2 tandem-seat trainer. Most nations are agreed that supersonic trainers of this calibre are economically not worthwhile unless they can also occupy a place in the front-line inventory. On the other hand there are dual-pilot versions of most modern combat aircraft, sometimes for training and conversion to the particular aircraft type and sometimes because a crew of two is needed to share the combat workload.

ABOVE *Designed as a Co-In (counter-insurgent) aircraft to quell dissidents inside Argentina, the IA 58 Pucará is a formidable attack aircraft against primitive forces, but it fared badly in the Falklands where the loss of 32 was admitted. This example was captured and is seen in Britain.*

Almost the only drawback to the F-111 is its high cost. This charge could not be levelled at the Vought A-7 Corsair II, which in 1964 won a US Navy competition for a successor for the A-4. Based on the F-8 Crusader fighter, the A-7 was deliberately made subsonic (slower than the speed of sound) in order to reduce cost and weight and carry more bombs further. Although a small and compact aircraft – popularly called Sluf by its pilots, standing for 'short little ugly fellah' – it carries more than 6800 kg (15,000 lb) of bombs and in Vietnam proved its ability to deliver them with pinpoint accuracy. It is a perfect example of the pure attack aircraft, lacking nothing in the way of navigation and weapon-aiming avionics (except for a TFR) and still retaining some air-combat capability with cannon and short-range missiles for self-defence. Like all US and British tactical machines it has provision for inflight refuelling, the Navy aircraft using a probe and the USAF version a dorsal receptacle for a telescopic boom.

As a contrast the Dassault Mirage 5 is a version of the well-known fighter in which a

Of course one attack aircraft with a two-seat version is the unique STOVL (short take-off, vertical landing) series of aircraft that stemmed from the pioneer Hawker P.1127 of 1960. This was the first vectored-thrust combat aircraft, in that the direction of the engine thrust can be altered by the pilot. Its Pegasus engine has four nozzles which can be rotated under the command of a single cockpit lever to point rearwards for thrust or downwards for lift, or even at the 110° position for inflight braking. The Harrier can therefore fly forwards, hover, or even move backwards.

Via an interim machine named the Kestrel, which equipped a UK/USA/West German evaluation squadron in the 1960s, the Harrier was developed as the first production STOVL aircraft in the world. It makes a short, rather than vertical take-off, in order to carry a heavier load of weapons. In addition to its two powerful 30 mm Aden guns it can carry up to 2268 kg (5,000 lb) of bombs or rockets externally and deliver them within minutes of a call for help being received by a local army unit. There is also a reconnaissance pod which can be carried instead of a bomb on the centreline pylon, and most Harriers have a reconnaissance camera in the nose behind the laser. The biggest advantage of the Harrier is that it can operate without needing an airfield. NATO air forces have in recent years tended to forget that they exist only as long as the Soviet Union declines to aim nuclear missiles at their small number of airfields. By having the facility to be somewhere

else when the blow falls, the Harriers might just escape destruction. A secondary advantage, discovered by chance by the US Marine Corps with its AV-8A version, is that by vectoring the nozzles in flight the Harrier can be made to perform manoeuvres other aircraft cannot do. This makes it a most difficult air-combat opponent, and at low levels a Harrier being chased by a hostile fighter can make a turn with engine thrust in such a way that the enemy fighter flies straight into the ground. 'Viffing' (from Vectoring In Forward Flight) may be a feature of fighters of the 1990s.

The Sea Harrier is described in the last chapter. The AV-8B Harrier II is a next-generation version which was developed by McDonnell Douglas in the USA and, because of a 1975 British government decision not to collaborate, has now had to be bought for the RAF. Planned for the US Marine Corps, the Harrier II is very strongly aimed at attack rather than fighting, and its new carbon-fibre composite wing not only has greater span and area, allowing room for much heavier underwing loads, but it also increases internal fuel capacity by 50 per cent. Numerous refinements enable virtually the same engine to lift an aircraft which weighs no more empty than the original Harrier, but which can carry either double the bombload or else fly twice as far!

In the RAF the new version will be the Harrier GR.5 (GR for ground attack and reconnaissance) and, although this US-developed aircraft does not meet the RAF requirements (for

There is little about the Harrier to show that it is unique—being the only tactical attack aircraft that does not need an airfield. This RAF Harrier GR.3 (GR, ground attack, reconnaissance) was actually the very first production aircraft. It was pictured on rocket practice in Sardinia, with RAF No 3 Squadron.

example, for speed and air-combat rate of turn) in the way the rival British Aerospace machine would have done, it is nevertheless a great advance over the original. The next generation beyond the Harrier II will certainly have much greater engine power, probably boosted by PCB (plenum-chamber burning) in which extra fuel is burned in the cool fan airflow, in a 'three-poster' engine with two vectored front nozzles and a single large rear nozzle on the centreline. With an engine of this type the future STOVL attack aircraft could be supersonic.

One of the most carefully planned attack aircraft is the Swedish Saab AJ37 Viggen, whose unusual tandem delta design was chosen to give good slow-flying qualities and fit the aircraft for operations from fields and country roads (because the Swedes appreciate the total vulnerability of airfields). The large augmented turbofan engine has a thrust reverser (to help pull up quickly on landing), and the tandem-wheel main landing gears are stressed for brutal 'no flare' landings like those made on aircraft carriers. Viggens come in other versions such as the SH37 and SF37 which, instead of 6000 kg (13,200 lb) of weapons, carry multi-sensor reconnaissance systems, the SH for use over the sea and the SF for land use.

Rather like the Viggen in having a single large augmented turbofan engine, and being produced in attack, fighter and trainer versions, the Soviet MiG-23 family (called 'Flogger' by NATO) have swing-wings for short take-off with heavy loads, good low-speed behaviour, modest fuel consumption and high air-combat agility. The MiG-23 has a tremendous Mach 2.3 performance at height or can attack at more than the speed of sound with the wings folded back. Many MiG-23s are dual-role fighter/attack aircraft, but there is a MiG-27 family intended solely for attack and with a different engine installation

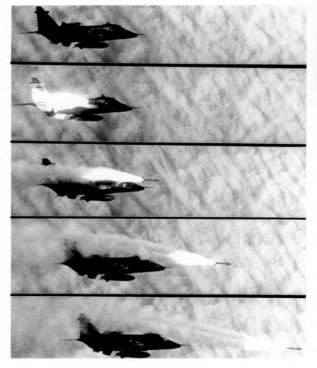

RIGHT *Just as fighters can drop bombs, so can attack aircraft fire air-to-air missiles or guns against other aircraft. This ciné film records the launch from an overwing pylon on a Jaguar of a Matra Magic close-range AAM.*

matched to high power at subsonic speed at low level. The engine, the R-29B turbofan, is basically the same as in MiG-23 fighters but has simpler engine inlets and has a smaller and simpler afterburner and less-complex variable nozzle. The nose, called 'ducknose' from its shape, has no radar but a mass of ground-attack sensors, and not only affords an improved view ahead but has thick armour around the cockpit.

Exactly the same shape and same engine was used by the Sukhoi bureau in creating the Su-24 (NATO name 'Fencer'), but with the difference that this formidable long-range machine has two engines. First identified in service in 1974, the Su-24 can carry a bombload of 8000 kg (17,640 lb) and has such a large fuel capacity it can reach the further parts of France or Scotland

from existing Warsaw Pact bases. It has much in common with the F-111 including a large nose radar (almost certainly backed up by a TFR), side-by-side seating, and swing-wings at the same level as the big slab tailplanes. Unlike the F-111, despite having fuselage-mounted landing gear, the belly can carry four large stores pylons, as well as two big cannon. About 600 were in service by early 1983.

An exact counterpart of the Su-24 is the Panavia Tornado which, despite being much smaller and having engines of only half the fuel consumption, carries about the same load over similar ranges. The Tornado is unique in being designed to meet the exactly specified demands of four customers in three countries: Britain's RAF, West Germany's Luftwaffe and Marine-flieger and Italy's AMI. It seats pilot and navigator in tandem and is the only production aircraft in Western Europe to have swing wings, which give it remarkable mission versatility, and in nav/attack avionics it is certainly the best in the world with the workload shared by two men with the most modern electronic displays. Experienced aircrew have said flying a Tornado is a completely new experience, devoid of turbulence or strain and for the first time enabling pilot and navigator to concentrate on the mission. The navigator in the backseat does most of the mission management, especially during the attack(s), leaving the pilot to keep an eye on the TFR which can be set to lower height and at higher speeds than any other aircraft in the world (1452 km/h/902 mph can be sustained at

ABOVE *White trails of vapour, caused by the reduced pressure in the centre of the swirling vortices of air, stream back from the tips of the small wing of a Jaguar GR.1 of the RAF No 226 Operational Conversion Unit at Lossiemouth, Scotland. It is carrying two 454 kg (1,000 lb) bombs and two drop tanks.*

RIGHT *Sweden's Saab AJ37 Viggen (Thunderbolt) was one of the first modern aircraft to have a canard (tail-first) layout, adopted to give good manoeuvrability and short take-off and landing. These Mach-2 attack aircraft are regularly operated from country roads, because the Swedes know the vital importance of being able to disperse airpower away from vulnerable airfields.*

sea level). About 140 Tornados had been delivered by 1983.

Not all countries can afford aircraft in this class, and, in a unique blend of Warsaw Pact and neutral industries, Romania and Yugoslavia have since 1971 been developing a small twin-jet called Orao (Eagle) by the latter country and IAR.93 by Romania. Resembling a less-powerful and simpler Jaguar, it first flew in 1974 and has since appeared also in a dual trainer version. Engines are afterburning variants of the Rolls-Royce Viper, each rated at 2270 kg (5,000 lb). Avionics have been bought mainly from Western suppliers, but few details have been disclosed. Development has been slow and apparently not wholly successful, and few appeared to be in service by 1983.

In contrast the Chinese Nanzhang Q-5, derived from the Soviet MiG-19 fighter of 1954, has been built in large numbers and even sold in quantity (42) to Pakistan. Compared with the agile and tough MiG-19 it has a redesigned fuselage with an internal bomb bay, extra fuel between side inlet ducts and a cockpit moved forward and closed by a clamshell canopy faired into a dorsal spine leading to the taller fin. The pointed nose contains attack sensors, and the bombload has been greatly increased to eight 250 kg (550 lb) bombs plus two large drop tanks, which together with powerful 30 mm guns makes this a hard-hitting aircraft.

Perhaps the hardest-hitting aircraft of all is the USAF's Fairchild Republic A-10A Thunderbolt II, designed in 1969–71 to meet a need for a close-support attack aircraft with special capability against armour. High performance was not called for, and the A-10A is much slower than World War 2 fighters and seldom exceeds 550 km/h (340 mph) in operation. It was designed around the 30 mm GAU-8/A, the most powerful gun ever put into an aircraft (although not the largest calibre). It fires armour-piercing shells at up to 4,200 per minute at such a high velocity they can pierce the top of any tank.

The large fuel-filled fuselage of the A-10A carries the twin turbofan engines high at the rear exhausting between the twin fins, and rides on a completely unswept long-span wing whose most challenging tasks are to lift the aircraft off short rough front-line airstrips with 11 pylons burdened with up to 7258 kg (16,000 lb) of

RIGHT *Most important Soviet attack and fighter aircraft today, the MiG-23 (called 'Flogger' by NATO) has a high-mounted swing wing and thus combines short field length with a top speed over Mach 2. There are many versions; these MiG-23s of the Libyan air force are carrying four AA-2-2 missiles in the air-combat role.*

LEFT *Most formidable of today's Warsaw Pact tactical aircraft, the Su-24 'Fencer' combines high performance, very heavy bombload and great range. The 600 in service can strike as far as the Western Isles of Scotland. Each is 50 per cent more powerful than the generally similar Tornado.*

ABOVE *Here seen in its element, at full power at low level, the Panavia Tornado is the most important attack aircraft in NATO. It was created by the joint effort of companies in Britain, West Germany and Italy to meet the needs of the three air forces and the West German naval air arm. At low level it is the world's fastest aircraft, able to maintain a speed of over 1450 km/h (900 mph).*

OPPOSITE TOP *The AV-8B Harrier II, developed by McDonnell Douglas of the USA from the original British Harrier, could be the most important single military aircraft of the next decade. In any future major war, the first things to be destroyed would be the airfields, and everything on them. The Harrier alone could survive, by being somewhere else; it can take off with heavy bombloads (seen here, 16 Mk 82 bombs) from a small ship, large truck or forest clearing.*

weapons and then pull tight turns at very low level. More than any other aircraft the A-10A is designed to survive hostile ground fire, and apart from a hit by a missile there is not much that can shoot it down. But attack pilots have a saying: 'AAA (anti-aircraft artillery) is 20 per cent lethal, SAMs (surface-to-air missiles) are perhaps 40 per cent lethal, but the ground is always 100 per cent', and many A-10As have been lost by flying into the ground during arduous low-level battle training.

A close Soviet parallel is the Su-25, called 'Frogfoot' by NATO. This is faster and longer and has the engines below the wing, but flies the same close-support missions in proximity to the enemy. It has been extensively and effectively used against tribesmen in Afghanistan.

Newest of the West's attack aircraft is a remarkably ordinary aircraft, and therein lies its strength. The AMX is being developed jointly by Aeritalia and Aermacchi in Italy and EMBRAER, the young aircraft company of Brazil. In many ways it resembles a jet fighter of the 1950s, in that it is similar to (for example) a Hunter in size, weight, power, speed and general capability. It differs in being far more modern in concept, the subsonic speed being chosen for the same reason as in the rather similar American A-7: to carry more bombs, further, using shorter airstrips. Another reason is to reduce

Panavia Tornado IDS
Countries of origin: Jointly by Britain, West Germany and Italy.
Dimensions and weights: Wingspan, 25°: 13·9 m (45 ft 7¼ in), 68°: 8·6 m (28 ft 2½ in); length 16·7 m (54 ft 9½ in); maximum loaded weight 26490 kg (58,400 lb).
Engines: Two 7258 kg (16,000 lb) Turbo-Union RB.199 Mk 101 augmented turbofans.
Maximum speed: 2124 km/h (1,320 mph).
Range: 3,895 km (2,420 miles).
Military load: Two 27 mm guns plus 8165 kg (18,000 lb) of external weapons.

risk and – important in an inflationary world – cost. A supersonic attack aircraft would cost much more, be much heavier, burn more fuel, and in fact would be unlikely to fly any faster at the treetop heights where it matters. The AMX is powered by a Rolls-Royce Spey turbofan, again a far from new engine but the best all-round choice on grounds of price, reliability, economy and ability to fly the mission. As well as an M61 six-barrel cannon, the AMX will carry 3800 kg (8,380 lb) of weapons and it should prove an extremely agile, efficient and useful aircraft. First flight is due in 1984 and delivery of 187 to Italy and 100 to Brazil (and without doubt others as exports) is to begin in 1987.

The remaining attack aircraft, apart from helicopters (see next chapter), are those derived

McDonnell Douglas/BAe AV-8B Harrier II
Countries of origin: USA and UK.
Dimensions and weights: Wingspan 9·25 m
(30 ft 4 in); length 14·12 m (46 ft 4 in);
maximum loaded weight 13495 kg (29,750 lb).
Engine: One 9979 kg (22,000 lb) Rolls-Royce
F402-406 (Pegasus 11-21) vectored turbofan.
Maximum speed: 1083 km/h (673 mph).
Range: Ferry range 5327 km (3,310 miles).
Military load: One 25 mm gun with 300
rounds (Harrier GR.5, two 30 mm) plus up to
7711 kg (17,000 lb) of external ordnance
including all tactical bombs, rockets and
surface-attack or anti-ship missiles.

from advanced trainers. Some, in fact, are even
light piston or turboprop machines; one of the
most successful is the Italian SIAI-Marchetti
SF.260 Warrior, which looks like a modern
lightplane but carries various gun and bomb/
rocket loads and has been sold to many air
forces. The same company builds the SIAI-
Marchetti S.211, smallest of the current jet
trainers yet available with a wide range of
attack loads up to 600 kg (1,322 lb) on four wing
pylons. Most of the trainer/attack jets are more
powerful. Yet another Italian machine, the
MB.339K Veltro (Greyhound), is based on the
MB.339A and MB.326 jet trainers but is actually
a single-seater; and there are single-seat attack
versions of many other trainers.

The two leading contenders are the Dassault-
Breguet/Dornier Alpha Jet NGEA (new generation attack trainer, initials in French) and the
100-Series British Aerospace Hawk, which can
in fact fly faster than its rival and carry heavier
loads, and has the advanced nav/attack system
based on that of the American F-16 (see page 41),
with Hotas pilot and backseat controls, inertial
navigation, laser ranger and large field of view
HUD (head-up display). It is remarkable that
aircraft of this calibre should have attack capability many times greater than much larger
aircraft designed from the start for the attack
mission in the previous generation.

Fairchild Republic A-10A Thunderbolt II
Country of origin: USA.
Dimensions and weights: Wingspan 17·53 m
(57 ft 6 in); length 16·26 m (53 ft 4 in);
maximum loaded weight 22680 kg (50,000 lb).
Engines: Two 4112 kg (9,065 lb) General
Electric TF34-100 turbofans.
Maximum speed: Clean, 706 km/h (439 mph).
Range: Ferry range, 3949 km (2,454 miles).
Military load: One 30 mm high-power gun
with 1,174 rounds plus 7258 kg (16,000 lb) of
external weapons on 11 pylons including all
tactical bombs, rockets and missiles.

BELOW *The Fairchild A-10A
Thunderbolt II was designed
to give the USAF a close-
support aircraft of devastating
effectiveness. Its weapons
comprise the most powerful
gun ever fitted to an aircraft
(the muzzle is visible) and 11
underwing pylons for all
kinds of missiles, rockets and
bombs.*

BATTLEFIELD HELICOPTERS

ABOVE *Bell Helicopter produced the AH-1 HueyCobra as a company venture and immediately sold it in very large numbers to the US Army and Marine Corps— and later to export customers. It was the first mass-produced battlefield 'gunship' helicopter for armed escort, defence suppression and anti-armour operations.*

PRECEDING PAGES *In exercise Bright Star '82 the new UH-60A Black Hawks of the US Rapid Deployment Force made 1,107 landings in Egypt, 777 of them in the desert. In actual warfare a heli-borne landing in such an exposed position would be fraught with danger.*

Helicopters took far longer than aeroplanes to mature as useful vehicles, and longer still to become viable weapons of war. As noted in the next chapter, they proved especially useful in maritime applications, but on the battlefield their ability as transports able to hover, or land on a small area, or pick up and relocate such items as artillery or light vehicles, or bring back casualties from the front line, all combined to overcome their basically poor range and speed, and vulnerability. Since the late 1950s special anti-armour or escort helicopters have formed a sub-group without an interior cabin, but bristling with sensors and weapons for use against tanks and other ground targets.

Like the aeroplane, the helicopter was transformed by the gas-turbine engine, which brought more power for less weight, less-volatile fuel, reduced vibration and dramatically improved reliability. The first production turbine helicopter was the little French Alouette II, of 360 hp and introduced in 1955. Built like the piston-engined Bell 47 (familiar to TV viewers of *MASH*) with a transparent bubble cockpit, it

differed from the earlier type in being able to lift five men or four anti-tank guided missiles. More than 1,300 were built, followed by over 1,450 of the Alouette III version with a streamlined seven-seat fuselage and 870 hp engine. This in turn was developed into the even more shapely and much faster Gazelle, exported all over the world; today it is the French Army anti-armour helicopter with six anti-tank missiles.

This best-selling family was launched in 1955, and a year later Bell Helicopter Company of Texas flew a new helicopter, the XH-40, which launched a family built in even greater numbers (believed to outnumber all other aircraft since 1945). Like all the most successful aircraft, this family has proved capable of extraordinary development. The XH-40 had a single Lycoming T53 turbine of 620/640 hp; today's Bell 214ST, the latest version, has two engines of 1,624 hp each. Whereas the XH-40 had a maximum loaded weight of 2631 kg (5,800 lb) and could carry a useful load of 454 kg (1,000 lb), the 214ST can take on board eight times this amount and lift off at a weight of 7938 kg (17,500 lb). In

avionics for retaining their attack capability in bad weather and against modern enemies. Some Cobras have twin engines, like many Hueys.

In Vietnam vast numbers of transport Hueys and gunship Cobras were partnered by the Hughes OH-6A Cayuse, more often called the Loach, from its designation LOH (light observation helicopter). Powered by a 317 hp turbine, this extremely compact tadpole-like machine was ordered for the US Army in 1962. Intended for battlefield reconnaissance, it blossomed forth as a six-seat transport, armed escort, defence-suppression helicopter and in many other roles. From it were developed nine different types of Hughes 500M or 500MD Defenders, some of which are burdened by a wide range of special avionics and weapons including the latest anti-tank guided missiles, rapid-fire cannon and Stinger air-to-air missiles for shooting down hostile aircraft. Another US type in the same class is the Bell 206 (OH-58 Kiowa), also called the JetRanger. The US Army bought 2,200 of these to follow the Hughes OH-6A, and is now likely to spend over $2,000 million having 578 of them rebuilt with a new four-blade rotor, a 650 hp engine and completely new avionics and weapons, with the designation Bell 406.

Small helicopters in the Warsaw Pact countries are the responsibility of WSK-Swidnik of Poland, where developments of the Soviet Mi-2 twin-turbine nine-seater have led to the 13-seat W-3 Sokol flown in 1979. In Western Europe great success has been achieved by the German MBB BO 105, powered by two 420 hp Allison engines and seating up to five. It is especially noteworthy for its manoeuvrability and lavish equipment, and one of many military customers is the German Army which has 212 used in the anti-tank role carrying three missiles on each side. Exactly the same twin engines are used in

ABOVE Much smaller yet faster than the HueyCobra, the Hughes MD 500 Defender has proved a bestseller in many versions. This is the latest, with an MMS (mast-mounted sight) above the rotor so that the helicopter can guide Tow missiles towards enemy armour while staying hidden.

between the two came well over 15,000 helicopters broadly known as the Huey family from the original military designation of HU-1 for 'helicopter, utility' (changed in 1962 to UH-1). The family was made up mainly of machines of about 4309 kg (9,500 lb) loaded weight, carrying 12 troops or six litter (stretcher) casualties, but many were equipped with radar and anti-submarine weapons for naval missions.

However, in 1965 Bell (by this time called Bell Helicopter Textron) had begun development of the first of the 'gunships'. Although it retained the T53 engine and rotors of the UH-1C, the new AH-1 HueyCobra introduced a slim fuselage like that of a fighter, with a cockpit seating a co-pilot/gunner in front and the pilot at the rear, at a higher level. Small wing-like weapon carriers on each side could fire clusters of rockets, machine guns or cannon and various types of anti-tank guided missile, while the speed and manoeuvrability of what was soon just called the Cobra were of a wholly new order. Mass produced for the Vietnam war, Cobras remain in production today in new versions packed with

ABOVE *Britain's Westland Lynx is certainly the best multi-role helicopter available in army and navy forms, as well as in the specialized versions shown on these pages. On this page is the Lynx 3 anti-tank version, heavier and more powerful than earlier types, carrying an exceptional load of anti-tank missiles including reloads inside the cabin, aimed via a mast-mounted sight (the spherical structure above the rotor).*

the Italian Agusta A109A, which is one of the fastest and best-looking light helicopters with fully retractable landing gear. The A109A has been developed in seven special versions for military, naval and police use, including one with four or eight anti-tank missiles. Agusta has now developed the much more powerful A129 gunship, with two 952 hp Rolls-Royce engines and a variety of missiles and other weapons.

By far the most important helicopter of British design is the Westland Lynx, also mentioned in the maritime aircraft chapter. The Army Lynx has skid landing gears and has been developed with more different types of battlefield equipment than any other helicopter, including seven types of rocket and missile and very comprehensive EW (electronic warfare) devices, mainly to improve its survivability.

To show the variety of tasks that can be undertaken by a modern tactical helicopter, the Lynx can carry a crew of two and ten armed troops, or teams equipped with Milan portable anti-tank missiles, or eight anti-tank missiles ready to fire, plus another six or eight in the cabin as a reload. Alternatively, it can carry various loads of mines plus automatic dispensers, or flares and a powerful 76 m (250 ft) powered hoist for rescue missions, or up to 14 items of reconnaissance and surveillance gear. Westland has now developed the Lynx into the Westland 30, with a cabin almost twice as large and with twin Rolls-Royce or General Electric engines of up to 1,625 hp each. These machines have flown with 24 seats, but would normally be used as long-range transports with only 17.

Large helicopters are extremely costly and are seldom flown into the thick of the battle, but the giant Mi-6 of the Soviet Union and the West's

Chinook and Sea Stallion or 'Super Jolly' are exceptions. The Mi-6 was by far the biggest helicopter in the world when it appeared in 1957, with a cabin similar in size to that of a C-130 or An-12 cargo aircraft, able to transport large missiles, armoured vehicles, 90 troops or 41 stretcher casualties. More than 500 of these monsters still serve with the Soviet armed forces, as well as a few Mi-10 crane versions with no ordinary fuselage but just a long beam carrying the cockpit at the front and tail rotor at the rear, and arranged to lift and reposition extremely heavy or bulky loads (but not to fly long distances). Today the new Mi-26 is in production, twice as powerful as the earlier giants and, like them, the holder of many world records. It is normally used as a cargo carrier, with a load of some 25 tonnes (55,116 lb).

Perhaps shortsightedly the West's HLH (heavy-lift helicopter), the US Army Boeing Vertol XCH-62, was cancelled in 1976 when the first was almost completed. Today money is at last being put back into this programme, and in 1983 an improved HLH may even be ordered. Powered by three 8,079 hp Allison engines it could carry external loads of up to 31.75 tonnes (70,000 lb), or possibly more. This compares with the limit of 18497 kg (40,780 lb) which is the West's record achieved by a US Army Sikorsky CH-54B Tarhe, the only crane helicopter outside the Soviet Union. Tarhes were said to have saved $210 million in Vietnam by bringing back more than 380 shot-down aircraft, but today barely 50 are in US Army service and they are very small compared with the Soviet monsters.

Numerically much more important, the tandem-rotor Boeing-Vertol CH-47 Chinook first flew in 1961 with two 2,200 hp T55 engines and is still in production today with later T55s of 4,500 hp. These extremely capable machines have a particularly convenient long cabin with a level floor at the same height above the ground as an army truck, and with a full-width ramp door at the rear for driving in vehicles. On one occasion 147 refugees were flown to safety in a single Chinook, and in the Falklands campaign an RAF Chinook (the only one to escape from the doomed ship *Atlantic Conveyor*) performed the expected work of five in some of the worst winter blizzards in flying experience. The Sikorsky S-65, called Sea Stallion or, in its avionics-packed HH-53H rescue version the 'Super Jolly', is in the same class as the Chinook, but not the equal of the three-engined navy versions described in the next chapter.

Only three or four nations today use helicopters in this class, partly because of the great cost. For most countries the top limit is the familiar S-61 Sea King, which is made under licence by Westland in Britain in special land-warfare models called Commandos. Although these have a water-tight hull with a planing bottom, they are not intended to be amphibious and lack the stabilizing floats of Sea Kings. Instead they have simple twin-wheel main land-

ing gears on which can be mounted various gun, rocket or missile installations to help suppress enemy fire in the armed assault role. Many Commandos have been sold to desert operators and have large sand filters in front of the engine inlets. The normal load is 28 troops or up to 2630 kg (8,000 lb) of cargo slung externally. On the first day they were used in the Falklands, seven Sea King HC.4 (Royal Navy name for the Commando) helicopters carried 520 troops and 454 tonnes (1 million pounds) of cargo.

The French counterpart to the Sea King is the three-engined Super Frelon, some of which have been used intensively in land warfare by such countries as South Africa and Israel. Larger numbers have been sold of the Aérospatiale Puma and Super Puma, which have the power of a Sea King applied to a more compact helicopter specially designed for battlefield missions, typically carrying 20 troops or a slung load of 3200 kg (7,055 lb). The Warsaw Pact counterpart, rather larger and made in vast numbers (at least 8,000), is the Mil Mi-8, which can carry 28 troops or small vehicles and in some versions has devastating air/ground armament, such as a heavy machine gun in the nose, four advanced self-homing anti-tank missiles and as many as

BELOW *The Westland 30 combines the engines and rotors of the Lynx with a much more capacious fuselage able to carry up to 17 troops with their kit.*

ABOVE The Soviet Mil design bureau has created not only the world's largest helicopters but also a range of large twin-turbine machines, heavier and more powerful even than the Sea King, which have been made in vast numbers. Over 8,000 were built of the Mi-8 and -17 transport and assault machines. This Mi-24 armed helicopter now exists in many versions of which at least 1,200 have been delivered.

RIGHT Developed as a more powerful successor to the HueyCobra, the Hughes AH-64 Apache has taken so long to develop its price has soared with inflation. No previous helicopter has ever deployed such advanced weapons or been so immune to enemy gunfire.

192 rockets, all carried at the same time!

Yet despite this Mil has designed a special gunship helicopter, the Mi-24, with even more air/ground sensors and advanced weapons, the entire nose being filled with radar, laser, infrared, advanced optics or low-light TV systems, as well as multi-barrel cannon in various turrets or side packages. Mi-24s, called 'Hind' by NATO, were first seen in 1974 and today are fighting with brutal effectiveness in Afghanistan. Its Western counterpart, the US Army Hughes AH-64 Apache, has been ten years under development, during which time its cost has soared, and is expected to enter service in February 1984. It is roughly in the same size and power class as the Mi-24, but has no interior cabin for troops or cargo and thus is a pure gunship. Its primary armament comprises 16 laser-guided missiles.

Surprisingly, the AH-64 packs all its many sensors into the tip of the low-positioned nose. This is surprising because to use them the helicopter must rise above any cover, so that it becomes fully visible to the enemy. As early as 1965 it was realized that any battlefield helicopter is only as good as its sights, which must provide a clear magnified view of targets, by day or night, and if possible penetrating fog, snow or smoke. The latest helicopters have an MMS (mast-mounted sight) carried above the hub of the rotor. Thus the crew can watch the enemy and guide missiles while keeping their vulnerable machine hidden behind cover.

Newest US Army helicopter actually in service, the Sikorsky UH-60 Black Hawk is in the class of the Westland 30 or Puma, with two 1,560 hp GE engines and seats for a crew of three and 11 troops. Many more could be lifted but the UH-60 has to fit inside a C-130 cargo aircraft and can also carry a heavy load of avionics or weapons, and self-protecting EW systems such as chaff (small strips of metal released to obliterate pictures on enemy radars), and IR jammers (which decoy heat-seeking missiles). Production is now also beginning on the EH-60A electronic warfare model to disrupt enemy radio communications and the HH-60D Night Hawk armed rescue version.

For 25 years many companies have been building VTOL (vertical take-off and landing) aircraft able to fly faster than helicopters, but except for the Harrier and Soviet Yak-36MP none has been successful. But in 1977 Bell began flying the XV-15 with rotors which can be tilted down to act like giant propellers on the tips of a wing, to enable a speed of 555 km/h (345 mph) to be achieved. Bell and Boeing Vertol are now trying to build a bigger tilt-rotor machine to serve as a Marine assault transport, Army EW and special mission aircraft, and Air Force search/rescue machine. This might herald a new era.

Hughes AH-64A Apache
Country of origin: USA.
Dimensions and weights: Main-rotor diameter 14·63 m (48 ft 0 in); length of fuselage 14·97 m (49 ft 1½ in); maximum loaded weight 8006 kg (17,650 lb).
Engines: Two 1,536 shp General Electric T700-700 turboshaft engines.
Maximum speed: 309 km/h (192 mph).
Range: 1804 km (1,121 miles).
Military load: One 30 mm gun with 1,200 rounds, plus four pylons for 16 Hellfire anti-tank missiles or 76 rockets or other weapon combinations.

BELOW *Sikorsky developed the UH-60A Black Hawk as the new combat assault helicopter of the US Army, and expects to deliver 1,107 of these tough machines, each of which carries a crew of 3 and 11 troops. By late 1983 a total of 420 had been built, and several other versions include the SH-60B (page 78).*

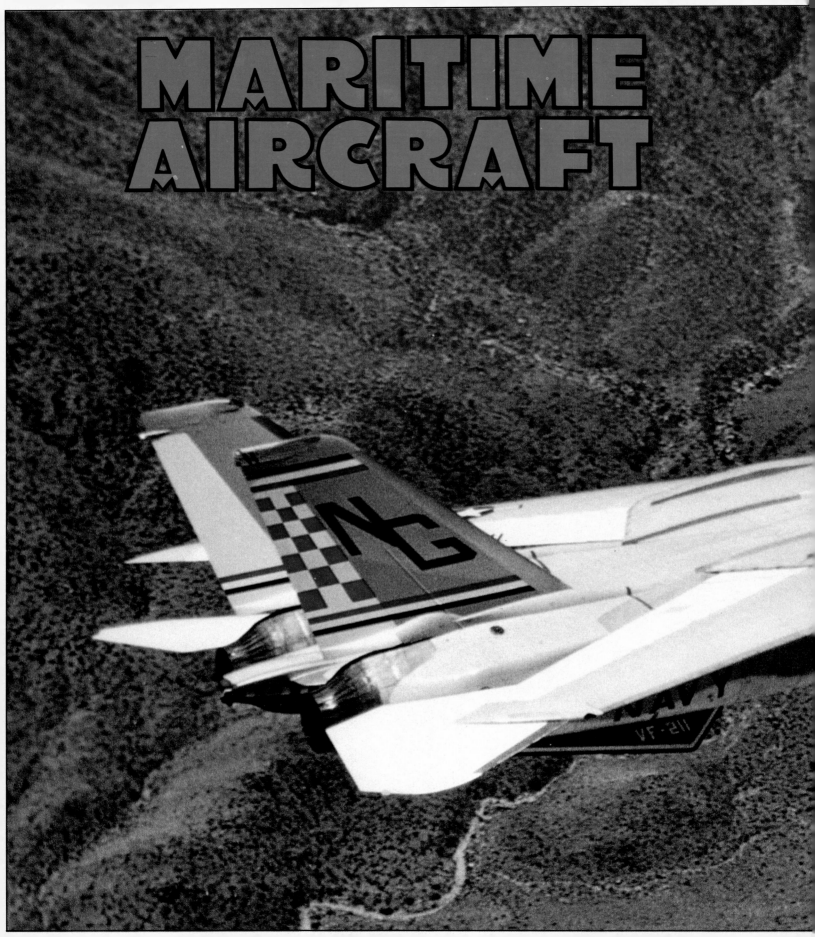

MARITIME AIRCRAFT

Maritime aircraft can be classified according to role, such as fleet defence, ASW (anti-submarine warfare), or long-range patrol. They also fall naturally into two distinct groups: those operated from shore bases and those designed to fly from surface vessels. The latter can again be divided into the fixed-wing types (aeroplanes) which demand an aircraft carrier and the VTOLs which can be part of the equipment of conventional warships such as frigates and destroyers. So far these vessels have carried only helicopters, but there is no reason why they should not also be equipped with jet-lift machines (although the Harrier family can carry a much greater payload if they can make a rolling take-off, which is not possible from ordinary warships).

In general oceanic areas are characterized by the large distances involved, so shore-based machines tend to be big and carry enough fuel for missions of long range and duration. Few contemporary aircraft can rival the capability in this regard of the Soviet Tu-142 ('Bear-F') ASW aircraft described in the first chapter. Perhaps surprisingly the American equivalent is a much smaller aircraft, the P-3C Orion, derived from the Lockheed Electra passenger airliner of the 1950s. To convert it for its maritime (primarily ASW) role a shallow weapon bay was added under the floor ahead of the wing and ten pylons for external stores installed under the outer wings. A great variety of bombs, torpedoes,

mines, depth charges, rockets, missiles and marine markers or buoys can be carried, up to a weight of 5443 kg (12,000 lb) on the wing pylons plus 3290 kg (7,253 lb) in the internal bay. Aft of the wing is a compartment packed with sono-buoys for detecting submerged submarines, and these are launched in various ways from tubes which are normally sealed when the above-floor area is pressurized. Nose sensors include a large radar and an FLIR (forward-looking infra-red to provide a picture of the scene ahead) detector, while at the tip of a long extension boom behind the tail is a MAD (magnetic anomaly detector). The MAD is carried as far as possible from the metal parts of the aircraft and measures the extremely small disturbance to the Earth's magnetic field caused by a submarine far beneath the ocean surface. Canada uses the Lockheed CP-140 Aurora, which is a P-3 filled with the ASW systems of the S-3 Viking.

The S-3, also built by Lockheed, is the US Navy's carrier-based ASW aircraft. It is perhaps the greatest-ever exercise in clever packaging, because the designers had to get as many ASW sensors, weapons and gallons of fuel as possible into a relatively small aircraft which could fold into the highly restricted dimensions imposed by the lifts (elevators) and hangars of carriers. Its stumpy fuselage seats a crew of four at the front, together with the specially tailored radar and retractable FLIR. Further back is a mass of

sonobuoy tubes, and in the tail is the same MAD sensor as carried by the P-3. However, in this case it is mounted on a long tube which can be extended far behind the tail when it is needed, just as the flight-refuelling probe can be extended forwards from the cockpit roof. The long-span high-mounted wings are filled with fuel as far as the oblique hinges which allow the outer wings to fold diagonally alongside each other. On the wings are hung the two turbofan engines and pylons for tanks or weapons to supplement those carried in the internal bay under the wing. The US Navy bought 187 S-3As, of which 160 are being updated as S-3Bs with extra data-processing, improved sensors and long-range Harpoon anti-ship missiles.

In the Soviet Union the standard shore-based ASW and maritime patrol aircraft is very like the American P-3, and is likewise a derivative of a turboprop passenger aircraft of the 1950s. The Ilyushin Il-38, called 'May' by NATO, was based on the Il-18 transport and closely resembles the P-3, except for the surprising fact (because its internal weapon bay is small) that it has no external weapon pylons. Compared with the Il-18 its wing is mounted further forward, suggesting a remarkable absence of equipment in the rear fuselage. Another Soviet overwater type is the unique Beriev M-12 amphibian, a versatile but elderly twin-turboprop used for general duties, although still fitted with ASW sensors and capable of carrying plenty of weapons.

Called Chaika (gull), these capable machines are good SAR (search and rescue) aircraft because they can alight in quite heavy seas.

Another amphibian is the Shin Meiwa US-1 of the Japan Maritime Self-Defence Force. Powered by four 3,060 hp T64 turboprops, these eight aircraft also have an additional 1,250 hp turbine whose function is to blow compressed air from slits ahead of the flaps, elevators and rudder to increase lift and control effectiveness down to speeds as low as 90 km/h (56 mph). Thus it can take off and land in distances of around 350 m (380 yd), and it can alight in waves of 4.3 m (14 ft) height, to rescue survivors. The related PS-1

BELOW *Like the P-3, the Soviet Il-38 was developed from a civil airliner, and the two types have much in common. This Il-38 was photographed with its rear weapon-bay doors open, dropping a sonobuoy into the Baltic during an exercise in anti-submarine warfare.*

LEFT *Standard fixed-wing ASW (anti-submarine warfare) aircraft embarked in US Navy carriers is the Lockheed S-3B Viking, which is packed from stem to stern with advanced electronics, systems and weapons. This pair is based on the carrier Dwight D. Eisenhower.*

flying boat is an ASW machine armed with homing torpedoes in underwing pods and many other weapons; 19 have been delivered.

In NATO European countries the most common maritime patrol aircraft in the 1950s was the US-supplied Lockheed P-2 Neptune. This wartime design is still serving in some parts of the world, and the Japanese built an extended and updated P-2J version with T64 turboprop engines boosted when necessary by underwing pods housing locally designed J3 turbojets. In Europe the task of replacing the P-2 was assigned to an international design competition from which the French Breguet Br.1150 Atlantic emerged as the winner. This efficient machine has a very large pressurized fuselage, a long-span wing with fuel for over 18 hours, and two 6,100 hp Rolls-Royce Tyne turboprops made, like the airframe, by a multinational consortium. A total of 87 of these capable machines was delivered in the 1960s, and now Dassault-Breguet is beginning production of a further 42 of the improved ANG (Atlantic Nouvelle Génération) type, with completely new sensors and avionics, and redesignated ATL.2

Britain used the Shackleton, derived from the wartime Lancaster, for many years, and still has one squadron of these long-endurance piston-engined machines in the oceanic radar surveillance role. As a replacement the totally new British Aerospace Nimrod was selected, the first of 46 being delivered in 1969. Unique in being a jet, this large and highly capable aircraft has the basic advantages of great range and endurance (with two or even three engines at flight-idling power), a smooth ride without the threshing vibration of propeller machines, the ability to cruise at high altitude at jet speed *en route* to a distant patrol zone, and unrivalled interior space for the normal crew of 12. Three Nimrods (designated R.1) were delivered as electronic intelligence aircraft, identified by their stumpy tails with small radars on the fuselage tip. The remainder were built as maritime reconnaissance aircraft (designated MR.1), packed with ASW sensors and with an enormous weapons bay which contains up to six rows of weapons including nine torpedoes. Sonobuoys are ejected from one of the rear-fuselage compartments, a MAD boom extends behind the tail, the main radar is contained in the underside of the nose, and the top of the fin houses an electronic-warfare installation. Today these aircraft are being updated to the MR.2 standard with

BELOW *The British Aerospace Nimrod is the largest, fastest and most capable of all long-range maritime machines, and today several variants exist. The most striking is this AEW.3 high-altitude radar surveillance model, with giant radar aerials at nose and tail, each covering a sector of 180° without obstruction by the aircraft itself. The inset shows the more common MR.2P ocean patrol versions.*

completely new sensors and data-processing systems, and many other changes including electronic-warfare pods on the wingtips. Yet a fourth Nimrod variant is the AEW.3 airborne early warning and control aircraft, with a powerful radar using unique aerials at nose and tail each scanning over a 180° sector. This radar is specially designed for overwater operation.

Nations with fixed-wing carriers, such as the USA, France, Australia, Argentina and, increasingly, the Soviet Union, can deploy seagoing fighters and many other types. The S-3 Viking has already been described. Fastest of all seagoing aircraft is the US Navy Grumman F-14 Tomcat, which with its swing-wing pivoted back at 68° can reach Mach 2.34 (2490 km/h, 1,547 mph) at high altitude. This tandem-seat long-range interceptor is powered by two Pratt & Whitney TF30 augmented turbofans which, despite their 20-year history, have given prolonged trouble in this application. The latest P-414A version of these engines is intended to do better, matching the tremendous performance not only of the basic Tomcat but also its AWG-9 radar and Phoenix missiles which can select six chosen aircraft from a close formation and destroy them all at a range of over 160 km

(100 miles). No other fighter can kill from such a distance, and another unique F-14 capability is to offer a choice of long-range air-to-air missiles (Phoenix), medium-range (Sparrows, later Amraams), close-range (Sidewinders) or a multi-barrel 20 mm gun.

Like all carrier aircraft the F-14 has to be engineered for a tough life. Each take-off involves a brutal pull by a steam catapult which, via a strong forged launch bar pivoted to the nose gear, hurls the aircraft off the deck at 240 km/h (150 mph) in $2\frac{1}{2}$ seconds. Catapult thrust exceeds 80 tonnes, and it would make no difference if the aircraft's wheel brakes were locked on. The pressure on the aft walls of the fuel tanks exceeds 23 tonnes per square metre (4,700 lb per square foot), and even the force on the bodies of each crew-member exceeds 1 tonne! Landings are even harsher, the heavy F-14 slamming on to the deck without the usual levelling-out (called the flare) in a landing on a runway. The wheels hit the heaving deck with the same vertical velocity as if the F-14 had been dropped by a crane from two storeys high! There is an 82-tonne impact due to vertical velocity alone, combined with instant wheel speed-up to some 230 km/h (143 mph), followed immediately

BELOW *Modern warplanes are complicated internally, but the Grumman F-14 Tomcat carrier-based interceptor looks complex externally as well. This dramatic head-on shot shows the wide spacing between the engines, the swing wings (here swept fully back) and the immensely strong landing gears for brutal deck landings.*

by a 55-tonne tug as the tail hook catches the No 3 arrester wire on the deck. Just to make life even tougher, as the fighter slams on to the deck the pilot swiftly opens the throttles to full after-burning power, ready for instant 'bolter' action to fly off again should the hook fail to catch the wire, or the wire break. So the hook not only has to stop the aircraft but pull it back within 2 seconds against the full power of the engines.

One can now see why the jet-lift V/STOL Sea Harrier is such a good idea. Harriers have operated from the smallest helicopter platforms on ordinary warships, and need no long deck, steam catapult or arrester gear. Nevertheless, as noted in the chapter on attack aircraft, the weapon load that can be carried depends on whether wing lift is added to the thrust of the engine at take-off, and a rolling take-off enables fuel and weapon load to be almost doubled. A further large gain results from ending the deck run in an upward-curved end section called a ski-jump. This imparts a large vertical velocity to the departing aircraft so, even if its Pegasus turbofan engine were to fail at the moment of becoming airborne, the pilot would still have plenty of height and time for safe ejection. Ski-jump ramps angled at up to 20° have been tested, the steepest inclination making the Sea Harrier oleo legs bottom at the limit of their compression. The ideal is 12° and the standard

take-off procedure is for the pilot to open up to full power with the nozzles aft, accelerate quickly along a short length of deck and go up the ramp, switching the nozzles to 50° as the aircraft goes off the end. This gives enough lift to keep an acceptable rate of climb while at the same time maintaining forward acceleration, so that the wing gradually takes over and the nozzles can be progressively moved back to 0° (horizontal).

Compared with the original Harrier, the Sea Harrier has a new front end with a neat multimode radar (which folds through 180° to reduce length for ship stowage) and a raised cockpit which not only provides space for many extra items of avionics, but also gives the pilot a good all-round view. Sea Harriers can do a wide variety of air-combat, anti-ship attack and re-connaissance missions, and demonstrated to the world their remarkable ability to fly around the clock in the world's worst weather in the Falklands campaign, when an average force of 22 (of 28 assigned) made numerous air/ground strikes on difficult targets, by day and night, and also shot down 28 Argentine aircraft without loss in air combat. The air-to-air weapons used were the American AIM-9L Sidewinder close-range missile and twin 30 mm Aden guns. Sea Harriers of the Indian Navy use the French Matra Magic AAM instead of the Sidewinder. It

BELOW *Victor of the Falklands, where it was dubbed 'Black Death' by the Argentine pilots, the British Aerospace Sea Harrier is the only aircraft currently available that can deploy any kind of tactical airpower with neither airfields nor carriers. Methods have even been worked out for deploying Sea Harriers from quickly attached pads on ordinary container ships.*

British Aerospace Sea Harrier FRS.1
Country of origin: Great Britain.
Dimensions and weights: Wingspan 7·7 m (25 ft 3 in); length 14·5 m (47 ft 7 in); maximum loaded weight 11794 kg (26,000 lb).
Engine: One 9752 kg (21,500 lb) Rolls-Royce Pegasus 104 vectored turbofan.
Maximum speed: 1191 km/h (740 mph).
Range: 3766 km (2,340 miles).
Military load: Two 30 mm guns each with 150 rounds plus varied external loads up to demonstrated limit of 3630 kg (8,000 lb) including AIM-9L or Magic AAMs and Sea Eagle or Harpoon anti-ship missiles.

is possible that a 'Sea Harrier' type conversion of the US-designed AV-8B Harrier II (see the attack chapter) will be produced, with other changes, to provide the most useful all-round vectored-thrust subsonic shipboard aircraft for the 1980s, although this would be slower than the Sea Harrier and possibly not so agile.

Of course, the main user of the AV-8B is the US Marine Corps, and the programme was severely delayed for three years – during which it escalated in price because of inflation – by the decision of the Pentagon officials to concentrate funding entirely on the rival F/A-18A Hornet. Many of these go to the Marine Corps, but they cannot be used unless one has either a large carrier or else a good secure land airbase. The F/A-18A Hornet was launched in 1975 as a lightweight low-cost successor to the F-14 and as a replacement for the F-4 fighter and A-7 (naval versions) attack aircraft. After intensive development it became an outstanding multirole single-seat combat aircraft, with the ability to carry heavy bombloads and deliver them accurately, to fight with an advanced APG-65 radar, radar-guided Sparrow missiles and a gun, and in the RF-18A version to fly mutisensor reconnaissance missions. The all-round capability is so good that Hornets have been selected by Canada, Australia and Spain, for use from land runways. The main problem is that,

far from being cheaper than the F-14, the F/A-18 is more expensive, and the US Navy Secretary was in late 1982 threatening termination in 1983. This appears unlikely actually to happen, but in an inflationary world a new aircraft type inevitably becomes less effective while its costs go through the roof.

It was partly to reduce risk and cost, but mainly because of nationalism, that the specially developed M version of the Anglo/French Jaguar was rejected by the French Aéronavale as a replacement for the Dassault Etendard attack and reconnaissance aircraft. In its place Dassault developed the Super Etendard, which looks almost identical and has a similar performance, but in combat capability is much better. A very ordinary traditional subsonic aircraft, it has a modest radar and non-afterburning turbojet engine, but does have improved nav/attack avionics. It also has the ability to carry a considerably larger bombload of up to 2100 kg (4,630 lb), although this is still limited compared with, for example, the 7711 kg (17,000 lb) of the AV-8B and F/A-18. The one effective weapon of the Super Etendard – as Britain discovered the hard way when she lost warships in the South Atlantic – is the AM 39 Exocet sea-skimming anti-ship missile.

These missiles usually dive from the point of launch to a height close to the sea where they are

LEFT *The TF/A-18 Hornet is one of several versions of the costly but very capable McDonnell Douglas multi-role aircraft now replacing the F-4 fighter and A-7 attacker in the US Navy and Marines.*

BELOW *Although it cannot make a heavily loaded rolling take-off the Yak-36MP, called 'Forger' by NATO, shows that the Soviet Union also understands the vital importance of jet-lift combat aircraft in maritime warfare.*

McDonnell Douglas F/A-18A Hornet
Country of origin: USA.
Dimensions and weights: Wingspan (without wingtip missiles) 11·43 m (37 ft 6 in); length 17·07 m (56 ft 0 in); maximum loaded weight 21887 kg (48,253 lb).
Engines: Two 7258 kg (16,000 lb) General Electric F404-400 augmented turbofan engines.
Maximum speed: 1912 km/h (1,188 mph).
Range: 3706 km (2,303 miles).
Military load: One 20 mm gun with 570 rounds plus up to 7711 kg (17,000 lb) of external bombs, rockets and missiles including Harpoon anti-ship missiles.

ABOVE *Considerably larger, heavier and more expensive than the Lynx, but doing the same job as a ship-based ASW and anti-ship helicopter, the Sikorsky SH-60B Seahawk is a version of the UH-60A. Note the 25-tube sonobuoy dispenser in the left side of the fuselage.*

extremely hard to detect by radar; in any case they are very small and are almost ideally shaped to give hardly any 'signature' on a defending radar screen. They navigate by inertial means (by precisely measuring all changes of direction and speed) or even by a simple autopilot, until they approach their target ship. Then a small radar in the nose of the speeding missile – occasionally an IR (infra-red) heat-homing seeker is used instead – picks up the mass of metal ahead and steers the missile into the centre of it, hitting just above the waterline. Sea-skimming missiles can be rocket-powered, for ready availability, or use turbojets for long range of around 100 km (60 miles), or a ramjet or ram-rocket for combined long range and supersonic speed. They are now the primary air weapon against surface ships, and of course cannot be used against land targets unless they are exceptionally prominent to a missile seeker.

Another old aircraft intended to be replaced by the Super Etendard is the Vought F-8 Crusader supersonic fighter. This Mach 2 aircraft gained a great reputation from the mid-1950s, but in the USA only a few photo-reconnaissance RF-8Gs remain with the Navy Reserves. France's F-8E(FN), however, must soldier on until the mid-1980s and certainly the Super Etendard is in no way a replacement, except to convert fighter squadron 12F to the attack role.

Britain's oustanding Buccaneer carrier-based attack aircraft has had to lay aside its sea boots and come ashore with the RAF, although one squadron will not be replaced by Tornados but continue in the maritime strike role over North Sea areas.

US Navy counterpart to the Buccaneer is the Grumman A-6, which differs in having a rounded nose filled with radar, side-by-side seats, engines under the long-span wings (which have full-span slats and powerful flaps) and all bombs hung on underwing pylons. The A-6, named Intruder, was also used as the basis for the Navy and Marines' EA-6B Prowler ECM (electronic countermeasures) aircraft. This detects, analyses and measures hostile radar and radio signals, tells the crew which weapons they are associated with (the most dangerous being fighters and SAMs, surface-to-air missiles) and then counters them by a barrage of carefully selected radio emissions called jamming. The EA-6B needs a crew of four and, while its receivers are mostly on the fin, its emitters are in large pods carried on what in the A-6 are the weapon pylons.

One of the more puzzling maritime aircraft is the Soviet Union's Yak-36MP, called 'Forger' by NATO. First seen in 1976 aboard the then-new *Kiev*, one of several fearsomely armed 40,000-ton warships deployed for open-ocean warfare, the

(840 lb) is the usual limit. Britain's Westland Sea King versions can carry rather greater loads, four homing torpedoes being the usual maximum. The Westland machines are equipped for more independent operation than the US Navy SH-3 models which rely to some degree on sensors and other facilities in the parent ship, which may be a frigate (only specially equipped ships can operate helicopters of this size and weight). There are many SAR (search and rescue) versions of Sea King, equipped with comprehensive navigation and communications systems, a 272 kg (600 lb) hoist and accommodation for about 22 'rescuees'. Most Sea Kings are amphibious and, although not intended for routine operations from the sea surface, can alight in reasonably calm conditions, in some cases using rapid-inflating bags for additional buoyancy.

The next generation after the Sea King in the US Navy is the Sikorsky SH-60B Seahawk, which though smaller is actually more powerful and can operate at weights slightly greater. Thus it is an extremely costly machine, and few countries will be able to afford it. Virtually the same job can be done by Britain's Westland Naval Lynx, which is much more compact and economical. Lynxes have been sold to many navies for either SAR or ASW duties, and they have no trouble operating from small ship platforms. The Lynx is just big enough to carry all the sensors, all-weather avionics and the weapons needed for versatile shipboard duties.

In the Soviet Union the Kamov bureau has for many years produced shipboard helicopters, whose compactness is assisted by having co-axial rotors that spin in opposite directions about a single axis. Like other machines in their category the various Ka-25 ('Hormone') and Ka-32 ('Helix') versions carry radars and anti-submarine sensors and weapons, but some models appear to be used only for the guidance of large missiles fired by submarines and possibly surface ships against distant fleets.

Yak-36MP is a jet-lift VTOL aircraft with two main-engine vectored nozzles aft of the stubby folding wing and two special jet-lift engines behind the cockpit between the main-engine inlet ducts. At take-off the lift engines direct their jets slightly to the rear, their forward thrust being balanced by having the rear nozzles rotated to the 110° position. Although the fuselage is long (and much longer in the tandem-seat trainer version) it has room for only a fairly modest amount of fuel, and all armament has to be hung on four wing pylons. The suffix initials MP probably mean 'maritime interceptor' in Russian, and one of the missions of the basic version seen so far is certainly the destruction of Western maritime patrol aircraft. Weapons include close-range missiles and gun pods, as well as bombs, rockets and possibly anti-ship missiles, but it is estimated that the total weapon load cannot exceed about 1500 kg (3,300 lb). With this aircraft STOL operations, with a deck run and ski jump, are not possible; thus there is a rigid limit to what can be carried.

In fact considerably heavier loads can be carried by some naval helicopters. Even the widely used Sea King, first flown for the US Navy in March 1959 as a future standard ASW machine, can carry various loads up to 2270 kg (5,000 lb) although in the ASW role the weight of radar and other sensors is so great that 381 kg

BELOW Workhorse of the Falklands campaign, the Westland Sea King serves in ASW (anti-submarine warfare), SAR (search and rescue) and assault transport roles. Here a pair of ASW Mk 2s fly home after an exercise in the English Channel (one almost hidden). Today's Mk 5 has a larger radar (the bulge above '50').

Index

Acknowledgements

The publishers wish to thank the following organizations and individuals for their kind permission to reproduce the photographs in this book:

Aerophoto Colour Photo Agency (M. Austin) 72, (C. Brooks) 12, 15 below, 28–9, 30, 31, 32–3, 36–7, 39, 42, 50–1, 77 above, (P. Little) Half Title, 75, (S. Wolf) 8, 16–17, 23, 68–9, 79; The Associated Press 27; Aviation Photographs International 8–9, 10–11, 14, 15 above, 58–9; Bell Helicopters Textron 64–5; Major Lennart Berns/Swedish Air Force 33; British Aerospace Aircraft Corporation 54–5, 56–7, 60, 74, 76; Central Office of Information 4–5; John Charleville, Sweden 20–1, (Swedish Air Force) 35 below, 73 above; Richard Cooke 46–7; Department of Defense, US Navy 58; Department of Defense, Washington 77 below; Department of the Navy, USA 38, 73 below; General Electric 26; M. Gilliat Title Page, 24–5, 61 below; Grumman Aerospace Corporation 44, 70–1; Denis Hughes 18–19, 34, 49 below; Hughes Helicopters Inc 65; Israel Aircraft Industries 37; Lockheed California Company Endpapers; McDonnell Douglas Ltd 49 above, 61 above; Military Archive and Research Services, Lincs 13, 22; Paul Popper Ltd 6–7; Rockwell International 45; Royal Netherlands Air Force 40–1; Saab-Scania Aerospace 35 above, 43; United Technologies Sikorsky Aircraft 62–3, 69, 78–9; Vought Corporation 52–3; Westland Helicopters Ltd 66, 67; Whitton Press Ltd (Ministry of Defence) 18, 68 above, (US Department of Defense) 59